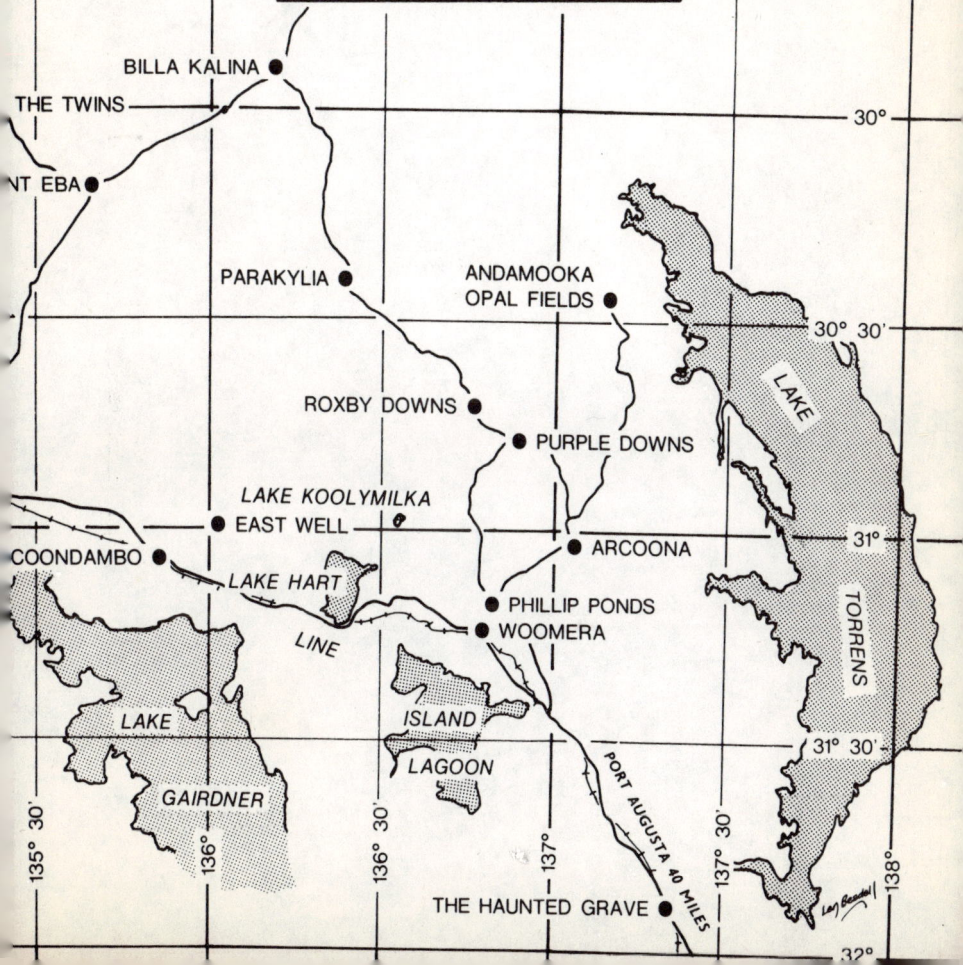

LOCALITY MAP

LOLLY'S TRIBE

29°

29° 30'

BILLA KALINA

THE TWINS

NT EBA

30°

PARAKYLIA

ANDAMOOKA
OPAL FIELDS

30° 30'

ROXBY DOWNS

PURPLE DOWNS

LAKE KOOLYMILKA
EAST WELL

ARCOONA

COONDAMBO

LAKE HART

31°

LINE

PHILLIP PONDS
WOOMERA

LAKE

ISLAND

LAGOON

GAIRDNER

PORT AUGUSTA 40 MILES

31° 30'

THE HAUNTED GRAVE

32°

LAKE

TORRENS

135° 30'

136°

136° 30'

136° 30'

137°

137° 30'

138°

STILL IN THE BUSH

Dear Barney,

Hope you like this book. The
outback is still there if you
want to come and have a
look!

All our love to you this
Christmas.

Graham, Helen, Scott, Blake & Liam

x x x x x

LEN BEADELL

STILL IN THE BUSH

LANSDOWNE

Books by Len Beadell:

Too Long in the Bush
Blast the Bush
Bush Bashers
Still in the Bush
Beating About the Bush
Outback Highways (a selection)
End of an Era

Distributed by Gary Allen Pty Ltd
9 Cooper Street, Smithfield NSW 2164

Published by Lansdowne Publishing Pty Ltd
Level 5, 70 George Street, Sydney NSW 2000, Australia

First Published 1975
Reprinted 1989
Reprinted by Lansdowne Publishing Pty Ltd 1994

© Copyright 1975 Len Beadell

Wholly designed and typeset in Australia
Printed in Australia by McPherson's Printing Group

National Library of Australia Cataloguing-in-Publication Data

Beadell, Len, 1923-
  Still in the bush.

  ISBN 1 86302 403 4.

  1. Launch complexes (Astronautics) - South Australia -
  Woomera. I. Title.

629.4780994238

Contents

*Train up a child in the way he should go; and
when he is old, he will not depart from it*

Proverbs 22:6

Illustrations

LEN BEADELL, who has been called the last of the true Australian explorers, was born on a farm at West Pennant Hills, NSW, in 1923. After showing an interest in surveying at the age of twelve under the guidance of his surveyor scoutmaster, he began his career on a military mapping project in northern NSW in the early stages of World War II. A year later he enlisted in the Army Survey Corps, serving in New Guinea until 1945.

While still in the Army after the war he accompanied the first combined scientific expedition of the CSIRO into the Alligator River country of Arnhem Land in the Northern Territory, fixing the location of discoveries by astronomical observations. Later, after waiving his Army discharge for a further term, he agreed to carry out the initial surveys needed to establish the Woomera rocket range. It was this decision that was to lead to a lifetime of camping, surveying, exploring and roadmaking in the vast empty areas of Central Australia, opening up for the first time more than 2.5 million square kilometres of the Great Sandy, Gibson and Great Victoria Deserts. He chose the sites for the first atomic bomb trials at Emu and for the later atomic tests at Maralinga.

As Range Reconnaissance Officer at the Weapons Research Establishment he was awarded the British Empire Medal in 1958 for his work in building the famous Gunbarrel Highway, still the only East–West road link which stretches 1600 kilometres across Central Australia.

In 1987 he became a Fellow of the Institute of Engineering and Mining Surveyors (Aust.) and in the same year astronomers at the Mount Palomar Observatory in California honoured him by naming a newly discovered asteroid planet after him in recognition of the road network he created which made access to the meteorite impact craters they were studying possible. In 1988 he was awarded the medal of the Order of Australia in the Queen's Birthday Honours list.

The author of six best-selling books about his experiences in outback Australia, Len Beadell is married and he and his wife have three children, Connie-Sue, Gary and Jackie — all of whom have features of outback Australia named after them.

GOVERNMENT HOUSE

ADELAIDE

SOUTH AUSTRALIA

FOREWORD

Mr. Len Beadell is still in the bush, delighting all who read his racy, amusing, yet amazingly informative accounts of his experiences in inland Australia. Those who have been bogged down in the mud, or isolated in the interior by floods, recently, will smile as they read, near the beginning of his narrative, of "the one or two showers of rain I'd receive throughout the course of a year." But Len Beadell writes magnificently of the near-desert area of the country, cruel and inhospitable, its sparse vegetation interspersed with red, gibber-covered soil which turned to choking dust when disturbed. There he surveyed and built roads and tracks, laid out a town and villages, prepared a testing site for nuclear weapons, made contact with aborigines living in a primordial manner, including one tribe unknown before he met them. His pioneering was done with theodolites and cameras, carried in motor vehicles and road-machinery, but it was pioneering in as real a sense as that of our ancestors. For him, it was an amazing adventure, tough, at times distressing, often seemingly impossible, but always recorded with meticulous care, and remembered with that abiding nostalgia which remains with all who have long experience of the aroma, the chill and the heat, the monotony and the variety, of the living desert of the interior of this isolated island continent. From all these, even from tooth-ache, Len Beadell draws inspiration. But, unlike the recluse who lives too long in the bush, he has bequeathed it all to us to share, vicariously, and because of his descriptive powers, almost as vividly as experiences of our own.

GOVERNOR.

1

An Unforgettable Meeting

The two Aborigines who had been crouching behind a spinifex clump stood up and with exaggerated boldness began striding towards me. They wore nothing but a matted string headband above which shot a disorderly shock of hair, and each clutched a bunch of long spears and a woomera. They were by far the wildest-looking pair I'd ever seen. This much I noticed at a glance as they closed the distance of fifty metres between us. As they stopped a dozen paces away, thrusting their spears into the sand, my hand fell from the butt of the revolver which I'd put on my belt. I would never have used it to harm them even if they had decided to throw the spears, but the noise of a shot into the sand might have been a deterrent; I'd had enough flat tyres for the day as it was.

I was 300 kilometres due east of Billanooka, one of the most remote cattle stations in central Western Australia. I hadn't seen another human being since I'd left the homestead weeks before, and so when I crawled out of my swag that morning I wasn't expecting to meet people. Later, as I watched them, I began to wonder which of us looked the roughest. Had these two men ever heard of Robinson Crusoe they might have thought they'd met him face to face. With my bare feet in hobnailed boots tied up only to the bottom two holes with kangaroo-tail sinews, and a ragged pair of shorts held up by a big belt with the bushman's "coat of arms" (watch and penknife pouches) attached, I probably looked more of a wreck than the approaching pair. A shirt which was only mostly there I had half-tucked into my belt with the torn part dangling, and with no water to waste I hadn't shaved since setting out on this lone expedition of 800 kilometres. Only lacing the boots to the first two holes was a standard procedure to make them easier to slip off dozens of times a day to empty out the sticks and spinifex tops which constantly poured into the funnel-shaped tops. I could also more hastily evacuate the occasional centipede which after the infrequent showers of rain would seek refuge in the boots alongside my swag as I slept. On special occasions, such as the time when the Duke of Edinburgh visited Woomera, I would relent and tie them up to the third hole; there were no spinifex tops on the red carpets upon which he walked.

The tribesmen stopped a metre or so away from where I stood near the Land Rover with its cluster of twelve-gallon petrol drums and spare tyres wired to the roof, and waited expectantly. I tentatively tried out the word of greeting, *palja* (pronounced "bulya"), which I'd learnt in the Pitjan-tjatjara country about 1600 kilometres away, and was rewarded with the grins which came immediately to their faces as they repeated it in reply. It seemed they understood some, if not all, of the language used by the people among whom I'd been working over the past decade. So with this encouragement I produced snippets of my repertoire, some of which brought results. I asked them if there were many with them in their tribe and informed them quite unnecessarily that I'd come from a long way off. The trouble with this procedure became all too apparent, for when they decided I understood their language, they started talking to me. This was another matter altogether, as they continued nonstop for half an hour at machine-gun speed. During this time I picked up one word every ten minutes, none of which bore the vaguest connection with the others. "Sandhill", "man", and "carry it", didn't at all give a fair idea of what they had been talking about. When they stopped, not in the least breathless, I hoped they didn't expect a comment from me. But in fact they seemed ready to launch into another spiel so I hopefully asked them about other members of the group I'd been studying through my theodolite telescope for the half day before. I knew that this would not have had the slightest bearing on what they'd been saying, and quite possibly I was ignoring some question they might have put to me just prior to the temporary halt in their recent harangue. It would probably be like somebody answering a person to whom they'd just been introduced with a "Good morning—lovely day", after that soul had opened the introductory phrase with "I murdered your grandmother this morning."

They took it politely under the circumstances, and acted as though they didn't even realise they'd been talking for half an hour to a brick wall. Instead they airily waved their hands about to the surrounding sparse mallee and balls of spinifex, a metre in diameter, separated from each other by completely bare sand. For half the day I had been waiting for this meeting to take place.

The night before I had camped nearly unconscious from tiredness in an almost full circle of jagged, high outcrops joining to the south a range of impassable mountains. Before I fell asleep I remember wondering how, if ever, I was to extricate myself and the Rover from them. That same evening at dusk, amid a cascade of smallish rocks, I had slid my Land Rover down into this depression on the western rim. From the narrow dry watercourse I'd been following for a kilometre or so I had not been able to see ahead to any great distance.

Once at the bottom I had no hope whatever of proceeding in any direction but further into the arena-like

3

enclosure two or three kilometres in diameter. I managed to stop short of a creek bed just over a metre wide, not quite as deep, but with vertical rocky walls. After sliding down the descent the Rover had come to rest in a position almost parallel with the gutter. The centre of gravity had been raised considerably by the four twelve-gallon oil drums full of petrol on the roof, and as the unfortunate vehicle teetered half a metre from the brink of the miniature ravine, I gingerly opened the door and climbed out.

With a geological hammer and shovel, I had managed after hours of digging and levering to put the four wheels on a less exciting plane. I used the rocks collected from this operation to construct a causeway upon which I eventually hoped to drive over the gully. As I dragged and rolled rock after rock, the vertical walls gradually took on the appearance of a rough inclined plane and in time the dry waterway had a sort of dam across it made up of rocks and bundles of chopped branches. This was a length in front of the Rover to allow room to turn on to it. At last all was ready for the attempt. There was an exciting moment when the front wheel slipped from the hard slope on to the loose material of the "bridge" and I involuntarily leaned further to the uphill side of the driver's seat in a completely useless effort to right the vehicle should it decide to topple. The action would have been as effective as trying to stop a waterfall with a barrier of wire netting, but as the other wheel found a footing, that particular danger passed. Next I had to gain what little momentum I could in the fraction of a second as the back wheels hit the crossing, to enable the Rover to scramble up on to the far bank. I had a feeling of firm friendship with the engineers who had perfected four-wheel-drive horseless carriages when at last the all-but-impossible crossing was behind me and I was on the eastern bank negotiating the thick scrub which often accompanies such creek beds. The rare times when water is actually present seem enough to encourage the dense growth of hardy bushes which can apparently thrive on only one or two waterings per year.

4

In the gloom of the starlight I had noticed the range to the south and the scene appeared the same to the north and east. Behind, of course, was the descent which cut off any thought of retreat, so I camped among the spinifex carpeting the arena's floor, not knowing and too tired to worry about how I was to handle the situation in the morning. I didn't even observe the stars for my latitude and longitude position because there were two staked tyres to mend. After the repairs I pulled the blankets and canvas camp-sheet over myself, blotting out all thoughts immediately.

To get to my present position on the western fringe of the Gibson Desert, 1300 kilometres due west of Alice Springs, I had worked my way from Ethel Creek Station, near Roy Hill on the Great Northern Highway, to Billanooka, owned by Bill Ellery, a real Australian bushman. Then I headed east from this rough but ready corrugated-iron homestead, thinking that Bill would be the last person I'd see for some time.

I was conducting another of my many solo expeditions, heading east to join the Gary Highway at its mid-point in the Gibson Desert, a road I had surveyed myself and made with my little "Gunbarrel Road Construction Party". This was a reconnaissance survey for the location of a new road in the 6500-kilometre network of access roads I had been making for the previous eight years. It would pass through the middle of the remaining virtually unexplored 2.6 million square kilometres of Central and Western Australia. The need for these roads became apparent as our rocket range project at Woomera and previous atomic testing ranges at Emu Field and Maralinga expanded, so that accurate survey information was needed to cover the whole of the range line from the launching pads north-west across Australia to the Indian Ocean. The Division of National Mapping was to carry out the geodetic surveys as a complete unit, using the network of roads my party and I were making, after close liaison between us as to the requirements. They would be following with work which would give calculations to allow for the curvature of the

5

earth, enabling instruments installed for either rocket or atomic testing to be linked up precisely with the main origins. This was of vital importance for recording the results of any test, as well as for the production of reliable and up-to-date maps covering areas of Australia which up to the present time had been shielded from everybody but Aborigines, by their absolute remoteness and inaccessibility. It took the urgency of a project of great national importance to initiate such a huge undertaking and the Weapons Research Establishment's Woomera combined with the Atomic Weapons Research Establishment's Emu Field and Maralinga filled the bill. The *really* "Dead Heart" of Australia was at last being made to reveal its secrets with the help of four-wheel-drive vehicles and bulldozers.

I was so grateful that I had been given the chance to start the work in this country that the physical hardships and labour connected with it were pushed far into the background, and I always considered it as a privilege rather than a job.

When daylight finally came on the morning of that eventful day, I was able to confirm my suspicions of the night before: I was apparently bottled up in a basin ringed by rocky mountains. There seemed to be a slight diminution in the escarpment several kilometres away to the north-east, and as it was the only possibility I made for it. I didn't stop to eat but just rolled up my swag. It was winter so the bed roll was covered with crisp white frost and would still be wet when the time came to undo it again.

After a kilometre or so a deep waterway began to take shape to the north and I followed it thinking it might wind its way to an outlet through the mountains. As the bed deepened to about 2.5 metres, several small water pools appeared, still full after some recent rain. By now I was driving slowly along its bank over the hummocks of spinifex. Some large ghost gums were growing on both banks a little way ahead, watered by what sparse rain fell in the course of each year, and I was forced to drive away from the southern bank for several hundred metres. When it was again possible to get near enough to see into the watercourse, I was met with one of the most pleasant sights I'd ever encountered in the Central Australian deserts. Crystal-clear rainwater, over a metre deep in places, stretched from bank to bank for eighty metres, the mirror surface perfectly reflecting a large snow-white ghost gum growing on the opposite bank. The reflection of the clear blue sky was broken by the line of green spinifex clumps lining the opposite bank, and the clean sand could be seen grain by grain on the floor of the pool, making the scene one I would remember forever. Here in one of the most remote spots in Australia, never before seen by white man, was a paradise, completely quiet on this winter's morning. I thought of how I'd camped so close to it the night before, feeling a wreck after the previous day's scrub bashing. This place was enough to erase all thoughts of that; as I had known in the past, the feelings brought by such finds are sufficient to last for the months if not years to follow battling with this harsh and inhospitable country.

I wasn't short of water. I didn't have to keep pouring it into the vehicle's radiator only to have it boil away as is the case in the hot months, and a billy-full a day was ample to drink. But an opportunity like this could never be bypassed, so I continued on to a break in the vertical bank where I could drive down on to the hard, moist sand beyond the pool and took the Rover as close to the waterline as possible. The first thing to do was to top up the sixteen-gallon water tank. With a tin basin I made a number of trips back and forth until the clear water in the filler tube was level with the top. The radiator came next, followed by myself, until at last, not having used a drop on anything as foolish as washing for many weeks, I was gasping for breath as I plunged into the icy water which turned my skin from a red dust colour to purple.

Back at the Rover I found a piece of soap which was more like a block of dry cracked wood, lying unused for so long in a galvanised-iron box I'd made for it. Rubbing it over me was a slow process at first as the sharp, hard edges

7

could have easily cut through my purple skin, but the soft rainwater finally melted it enough to give a few bubbles which I assumed from their golden colour had combined with the dirt. Back into the pool to get them off and renew the fading purple, and my bathing was over for another month or so.

As I pulled my old shorts back on I noticed a clear footprint in the wet sand. Further excited investigation revealed others of different sizes, and I knew that Aborigines had been right here within a day at the most. Thinking of the remoteness of the place I concluded that they must belong to a tribe which could be one of the most isolated in the outback deserts of Australia. There and then I determined I must try to make contact with them; it could be the most important discovery I would ever make. It might mean camping in the area for days until some sign of them appeared, as it would be useless to try and find them unless they wanted to be found.

With the fresh tingling sensation of the icy water still with me, I climbed back into the Land Rover and decided to explore the immediate vicinity for further signs, forgetting altogether that I was not yet out of this rock-bounded arena. Before getting to a place where the bank would allow me to scramble the vehicle up out of the creek bed, I noticed some exposed roots, revealed by erosion over the years. They had been broken as recently as the day before, probably by the owners of the footprints. As I followed the natural course of the creek still further, more pools of water appeared, smaller but equally clear, until finally the stream wound its way around the base of a rocky outcrop. I could at last see a skyline beyond the mountains, offering an exit for which I'd been hoping and searching since sliding down the stony descent the previous evening.

But it wasn't only the skyline which made me excited: so did the thin spiral of smoke which rose straight up in the still air in front of a sand ridge 300 metres away to the north. While I watched, the smoke alternately swelled into black clouds and dwindled to thin white strands, as I'd so

8

often seen when Aborigines hunting food lit spinifex fires to burn out the lizards which lived in the shade of the clumps. Here was real visual proof of the existence of this remote tribe who had made the foot tracks at the pool.

Driving in the direction of the fires past several brimming rock pools, the Rover slowly lumbered across the intervening spinifex and scrub country. In another quarter of an hour I was able to see a row of burning clumps, the smoke blackening as each successive hummock caught alight and blazed up in a small inferno of red-hot gum and spinifex resin. Aborigines melt and knead this gum on to the handles of their woomeras as a knob to grip while spear throwing. Often a small, sharp stone is embedded into the black mass before it sets hard, and is used as a kind of chisel in scraping the new wooden implements they make from time to time.

Then, within a hundred metres of the fires, I had a fleeting glimpse of the first human being I'd seen for many weeks. Between a gap in a clump of low mallee trees I saw a naked black form dart across, bent low, clutching a bunch of spears as he ran to the cover of some bushes. This was where I was going to stay and camp until I had actually made contact with them. I wondered what they must have thought, seeing this strange shape lumbering across the ground towards them; where had it come from, and why, and what did it all mean? My thoughts were not very different as I placed the Rover in a small bare patch of sand in case the fires came too close, and switching off the engine, I knew it would not be started again until these people had been contacted and, hopefully, photographed.

As I watched the spot where the first man had crouched, a flicker to the left revealed another manoeuvring further behind a shrub, but only partly concealed from me. Scanning carefully to the left and right I sighted several others, and even a couple of women scurrying up the sand ridge, half-carrying and half-dragging some little children, until they disappeared over the far side. It would be a long time before I could tell anybody about this exciting happening, I thought as I sat still, not daring to make any sudden movement for fear they might race off into the bush and sandhills to be lost again to the desert.

The sort of reception I would get might depend upon whether I was unwittingly trespassing on some sacred ceremonial ground, or too close to hidden tribal boards, but at the moment I was only intent on obtaining a reception, be it good or bad. Carefully opening the door of the Rover, I slowly climbed out, thinking what an eventful and unforgettable day of exploration this had turned out to be.

2

"Hairy Lolly"

I wanted to show the concealed figures that I was alone, so very slowly, I ambled a few paces clear of the Rover and casually looked about. More stealthy movements showed to the left and right of the first sightings, giving me the impression that there was a complete tribe in the area.

By then it was an hour before noon which gave me the idea of taking a latitude observation from the sun to plot the exact position where first contact with these people would be made. I didn't want to lose this spot in the desert if the subsequent hundreds of kilometres of reconnaissance survey made it necessary to locate my future road somewhere else. I walked back to the Rover and slowly unpacked my theodolite. I was sure that every movement was being examined by an unknown number of hidden pairs of eyes. It gave me quite an eerie feeling after living alone for weeks in the sandhills, far from normal habitation. To know they were there, unwilling to show themselves and possibly thinking that I was still unaware of their presence, made the atmosphere all the more strange. I screwed the instrument to the tripod which I'd carefully set up a little

11

in front of the vehicle, in a position where they could see me clearly. After some short calculations as to the local time of transit of the sun across my assumed meridian, I began scanning the clumps of spinifex and shrubs through the telescope. There was a wait of three-quarters of an hour to transit so what better way could I find to use the time than searching for an unknown tribe of Aborigines with the powerful lens. As I aimed the sights along the top of the tube towards the hummock behind which I was sure I'd seen the Aboriginal hiding, I moved my hand down from the eyepiece and felt for the focusing screw. Sure enough, as the image became clear it revealed above the spiky perimeter of the spinifex a tousled mop of black hair, below which showed the whites of the eyes. The end of a bunch of spears also poked out of the bush.

More pairs of eyes and spear-tips were revealed as I traversed the instrument and soon I discovered that I was completely surrounded. Turning the telescope to the sand ridge, the women and children of the tribe could be seen peeping over the crest. Through the inverted image of the telescope the sand ridge appeared at the top of the field of view with the sky occupying the lower half, and the row of heads seemed to be hanging down from the line of the sand. It produced a most awesome feeling with all these silent forms fixing me in a crisscross pattern of peering eyes, and no one making a move to be seen or heard.

The time was getting close to noon with the sun almost in a position for observation, so I temporarily left the study of my mysterious neighbours to concentrate on obtaining the latitude of this rather historic spot. Screwing a diagonal eyepiece to the telescope in place of the present one in order to see through the instrument at an angle as it pointed skywards, I began reading the angles until the sun had passed its zenith, then settled down to calculate the results. But I couldn't wait for just another peep at my newly-found friends, or foes, as the case might be, so I replaced the straight eyepiece and checked on the situation, finding it to be about the same but with the addition of several more heads.

12

I found the latitude to be 23°S, which put my position at eighty kilometres north of the east-west line through Alice Springs, 1300 kilometres away to the east. The date was 4 August 1963. After plotting this on my almost blank map, I again waited for something to happen. I hoped we would make contact within the week as my few remaining rations might not last much longer.

Several hours later, just as I was beginning to think I would have to settle down here for the night, I saw the first movement made with the deliberate intention of being seen when two of the men stood up and strode towards me. After that first meeting with their spears still stuck in the ground a little way off, we all sat down on the bare sand between the spinifex and continued the conversation with the aid of sticks scratching on the ground. I tried to find out if there were many in their tribe and to entice others over to our conference, but this was soon unnecessary as two more became curious enough to add their spears to the first lot and join us. No introductions other than my *palja* took place as the five of us sat in a circle and drew pictures in the sand to supplement our talk. My mind was on my camera in the Rover and I was waiting for a chance to use it. But any movement to the vehicle might, I thought, scatter the group for ever, so we pressed on with our exchange of whispers, which Aborigines often use instead of loud voices when talking to each other at times like this.

I tried to explain that I would be coming back with several larger vehicles to make a smoother road, and would have a few more men with me. After two hours of concentration the light suddenly dawned on one of them and he gestured wildly in the relieved action of one who has just had a great weight lifted from his shoulders, and launched into a rapid-fire explanation to the others of what we had all been talking about for half the afternoon.

One by one their faces lit up and I waited for the excited undercurrent of voices to ease before following up with my news. By then several others had overcome their shyness, but no women and children arrived. They still

13

remained on the far side of the sand barrier observing the proceedings. Deciding to try out some more words of what I hoped was their own language, I asked them if they could bring over some children, and was immediately rewarded by one old man standing up, raising his arm, and beckoning with his curled fingers pointing downwards. Whenever an Aboriginal beckons, he expects people to walk towards him on the ground, whereas white people, by aiming their forefinger upwards in their beckoning action, seem to think they can fly through the air.

This showed that he at least understood me, especially as he supplemented the action with a string of words, resulting in a woman with a toddler appearing over the sandhill and walking down on to the flat. Once there she bundled the child on to the ground and hurried back to her original position. One of our group walked over and returned with a very plump little boy about two years of age, with scars on his shins but otherwise quite healthy looking. I'd often treated similar scars caused by children rolling in their sleep on to their little fires in the winter, burning themselves before they woke up. The chubby appearance of his arms and legs may have been deceptive as this is often a sign of malnutrition, or an unbalanced diet which also gives a swollen stomach.

Now as he sat on the knee of an old man who hadn't moved from his original position on the sand, I thought I must make the move for my camera.

Standing up slowly, I moved around to the driver's side of the Land Rover, the only door I could open as the stores were piled against the other, and pointed out the handle to the people who had followed. They examined it from a safe distance and when satisfied it was harmless, their whisperings gave me the cue to actually open the door a little. Another reassuring pause, then I felt confident enough of their remaining with me to open it wide. This action was accompanied by audible and excited gasps from the audience. The rifle was something I must demonstrate, along with the revolver and also the short-wave transistor radio used for obtaining time signals for

14

longitude observations, but not before securing a collection of photographs.

I pointed to the strap hanging down from the camera case in its rubber-lined box and let that sink in, then I was at last able to take the instrument and place it on the seat. The interest focused on it was intense and, amid a cloud of flies, it was finally in my hands and being minutely studied at close range. One by one I encouraged each person to look into the viewfinder which I aimed at someone. When they saw one of their own group greatly diminished, it was too much for words, and the awed silence remained as I trained it on them and pushed the button. For the first time the images of these people had been reproduced on paper for the outside world to see. I hoped, as always at times like this, that the camera was still working. A picture of the chubby boy came next, followed by a carefully-planned close-up of an elder of the tribe to whom I'd been talking, or rather gesturing, for some time. He seemed to be the comedian of the group. After each exchange he would screw up his eyes, slap his bare leg, and fall to the ground laughing until tears rolled down his cheeks. While I was photographing him I noticed that he rarely looked into my eyes but darted most of his glances over my shoulder to something or someone behind me. I turned around to see what had been the cause of his interest.

The sight which met my eyes is one I'm sure I will never forget; it all but took my breath away. Face to face with me was the most unusual person I'd ever seen, black, white, or any other shade, in the form of an old Aboriginal, covered completely by a heavy thatch of hair eight centimetres long. His face merged into his neck with no line of demarcation, and hair covered his shoulders, chest, arms, and legs. An extraordinary feature about him was that the top of his head was almost bald, and the dense mat of hair started just below the crest of his skull. Although he had obviously never seen himself, when I stared at him with the flies swarming into my open mouth, he grinned at the effect he had on me, showing his face to have a very kindly and almost benevolent character about

15

it. The only thing I can think of to say was that at least you could tell which way the wind was blowing while talking to him.

It was going to be a long time before I could share this experience with anyone, but it was certain that this particular Aboriginal above any others I'd ever met would settle the topic of conversation for many years to come. But I would have to discover his name and this was the next thing to do before obtaining the set of photographs I was burning to take. I again tried out my limited knowledge of their language and asked him what his name was, and was astounded at the one word, "lolly", I received in reply. Telling him in English that I was sure he had never heard of lollies in his life I tried again, with the same result, so I produced a tin of aniseed balls which I had happened to get from a little bush store hundreds of kilometres back at Nullagine. When I placed a sweet in his hand I could see that he didn't know what on earth to do with it, so I put one in my own mouth. Immediately he did the same, swallowing it down in one gulp, with a sound like a stone being dropped into a lake. I began to tell him that he wasn't supposed to, but not knowing any Aboriginal word meaning "to suck", I said it was too late now anyway.

When I asked his name yet again, he stuck to his one word "lolly", so I gave him another. About a dozen aniseed balls later, just when I was thinking they were getting a grip on him, I discovered his name was "Lolly". He had been trying to tell me, but each time I had just given him a black marble from my tin.

During this "conversation", I had pointed to myself, and told him my name. In a last effort to convince me he had repeated it, immediately transferring his aim to his own nose and saying once more "Lolly". On listening very carefully I at last realised it sounded more like "Lourly". Then came the camera.

He was a rock-still model, and as he turned around for a side-on-view, the mat of hair covering his back became visible. His teeth were big and strong so I gestured for him to open his mouth. He obliged and the resulting picture looked more like a black cavern surrounded by bush, as I saw when, thankfully, these rare photographs came out perfectly, months later.

What a day to remember this had been! After a rough count there seemed to be at least forty in the tribe including the heads visible over the sandhill. I was quickly getting the feeling that these were the happiest and most contented group of desert people I'd ever had the pleasure of meeting. Totally unspoilt by white contact in any shape or form, for the most part appearing as sound in body as their far-off white neighbours, they had led their hard lives in complete harmony with nature for many generations.

The short-wave transistor radio came to mind at this point so once again we all moved around to the open door and I set it up on the mudguard, extending the aerial as I did so. This new object drew their undivided attention. I waited for their initial examination to be completed, then switched it on. The immediate effect was electrifying, as loud intakes of breath momentarily drowned out the voice of the announcer telling his listening audience the name of his next record. If only he could have known just who made up that audience! Then came the music which made them, as one, retreat a few paces before excitedly looking around to the rear of the small box and under the vehicle, completely perplexed. Each time I tuned it in to a different broadcasting station they set up a fresh hum of whispered exclamations, wondering how the voices turned from a man's to a woman's in an instant and how two people could possibly fit into the small box anyway.

The next item to demonstrate was my revolver. After a great deal of safety precautions and an attempt to inform them it had quite a loud voice, I fired a shot into a bare sandy patch. This was received, not fearfully, but with an excited ovation, shouts of laughter and wild gesticulating of arms. I happened to have an empty fruit tin used for pouring oil, so I put it upside down on a stick in the ground close enough to ensure a hit, and fired again after taking the most careful aim I can ever remember. I was relieved to see that the tin spun off the stick. Amid the renewed

17

yelling, one man even ventured to retrieve it and held it up to the rest for their inspection. As I watched the expression on their faces I thought how many Western inventions had gone into obtaining this result.

The demonstration of the rifle was even more impressive because the tin could be placed at a more respectable distance with an equally sure possibility of hitting it. When the target spiralled off once again into the air, it won them over lock, stock, and barrel.

The sight of one of their dingoes gave me a further idea for entertainment. Producing a notebook and pencil, I drew a sketch of the extremely bony dog surrounded by a mist of flies and gave it to them. This scrap of paper brought more genuine enthusiasm than all the other items put together as it was something they understood; I'm sure the roars of excited laughter could be heard by their womenfolk over the sand ridge. They didn't miss a thing on the drawing and when I borrowed it to add a goanna crawling from a clump of spinifex I knew I had friends for life.

One of the tribe, a young boy about eighteen, had a large hole in his nose in which to insert sticks or bones for special occasions. I tried to take a colour slide of him, a profile view against the white side of the Rover. He was quite willing to be placed at the right angle, not really knowing what was going on but sure that it wouldn't hurt, and remained rock still until I had pressed the button. In the viewfinder the glaring white background showed past his black features and through the hole. They punch the hole with a sharpened piece of bone or stick, then roll up a shiny mallee leaf which is pushed into the jagged aperture, keeping it open and round until it heals. The leaf is constantly rotated and when withered is replaced by a fresh one until finally the hole has set, open for all time. I asked one of men to place something through his nose-hole for another picture, and he broke off a small white stick and pushed it through. Before taking the photograph I straightened up the axis of the peg until it was parallel with the line of his eyes, as well as tapping it across until the nose bisected it. It felt as if it were set in a jelly and his face moved easily about during the operation.

Now that this meeting had actually taken place I thought I should press on with my expedition. Several hundred kilometres of unknown country lay between me and the Gary Highway which I hoped to be able to reach eventually.

I was sorry the rest of the tribe had remained hidden; later, when I again came into contact with them, this situation remained the same and I never really got to see the women and most of the children, except through the lens of my theodolite. Then I had to reluctantly leave them, but with the comforting knowledge that this spot, in such a huge area of sandhills, mountain outcrops, and spinifex, was accurately plotted on my map as a result of the sun observation. This meant I could return at any time to see them again, even if the country which lay ahead made it impossible for me to locate my future road in such a way as to bring it past the spot where this encounter took place.

One way or another, with or without the road, I was sure I'd be seeing them again, providing of course I could get through to the comparative civilisation of the Gary Highway myself, and I endeavoured to tell them as much. There were no such things as handshakes out here, so when they had finally gathered that some time in the future I would be back, I climbed into the Land Rover after returning the radio, camera, rifle, and revolver to their respective places in the cabin.

Giving Lolly a few special pats on his hairy shoulder, I started the engine. It was late in the afternoon by now and I could make at least a few kilometres before dark. What they must have been thinking as I slowly lumbered away I could only guess. As I shut the door, I mentally gave the pool in the creek bed, which was the start of this day's adventure, the obvious name of "Lolly Water".

3

A New Junction
is Formed

The events which led to the discovery of this remote tribe
had their beginnings two years before when I made the
statement "we are going to make a road now from here to
the Indian Ocean", "here" being a point on our already-
constructed Gunbarrel Highway. Our little party gathered
around as I pointed to the windrow on the northern edge
of our previous road across Central Australia, with the
huge low-loader truck carrying a bulldozer on its tray
stopped alongside. The Number 12 Cat. road grader with
its great diesel motor still idling stood behind, followed by
the long-range supply vehicle, the ration wagon and, as
usual on long trips, the fitter's lorry carrying spares for
everything and all appropriate tools, came last. Any vehicle
breaking down could therefore be repaired and if Rex,
who drove it, got into trouble himself, he could, with his
expert knowledge and travelling service station, fix himself
up. Nestled among the heavier equipment was a workshop
Land Rover full of other tools, oxyacetylene bottles, a
built-in vice on a tailboard converted into a bench, and
drawers of special sets of spanners, gaskets, emery wheel,

hacksaw, and so on. It would service any distant stranded vehicles. My Land Rover loaded with survey instruments and calculation books, radio transceiver, rifle, bed, and a separate lot of tools and spare parts, completed our convoy. With it all we hoped to make the next 2600 kilometres of road of our overall 6500-kilometre network.

Quinny, the long-distance supply driver, wanted to know what we were all standing about for instead of unloading the dozer and getting into it. We had all just driven from Adelaide, 2400 kilometres away, after repairing the vehicles from the previous year's desert work, and restocking for the new onslaught on this section of virtually unexplored and almost unmapped Australia. We would be working to the north through the Gibson Desert, and then diagonally north-west, right across the Great Sandy Desert of Western Australia, with a final road due west. This would add two more road links across Australia to the two we had already made, further to the south.

Doug was still driving the bulldozer, and the grader would look quite lonely and out of place without Scotty as operator. Wild horses couldn't keep old Paul away after being with us for five years already. He'd cooked under the most impossible conditions anyone could be asked to, with dust storms, ice in the water during winter, and boiling himself by his fire during the long, searing summer months. He never wore a hat, content to take shelter from the inferno of the sun by standing in the shade cast from his ever-present solid black cloud of flies. He still had his three rocks on the back of his ration truck, ranging in size up to the "forty-knot pot-lid rock" he used in sand and dust gales to keep his pots firmly down on the little woodstove we carried on a trailer. Before acquiring the weights, we once spent till midnight searching the near-by sand ridges in vain for our tea which had been swept off the fire by a wind storm that had hit the camp just as he was preparing the evening supper. However short of water we were, he always washed his left elbow on Wednesday and Saturday, and he used it to knock back the rising dough for breadmaking as he drove along. He would

21

prepare the yeast dough and put it in the wash-up basin, placing it in turn on the empty passenger seat of his truck near the warmth of the engine. As we shifted camp daily to the head of our road as it progressed, he would slowly drive his wagon pulling the trailer along, and throughout the short drive, he could keep his eye on the flour. When it rose past the rim of the basin he'd lean over and thump it down with his elbow without further slowing his snail's pace, and the dough would be ready for the bread tins at the new camp.

Eric drove the workshop Rover, doing a dual job of helping everyone do everything as well as "cherry picking" the finished road for odd roots and stones left behind after the last pass of the grader. This was necessary as they could stake our tyres during construction, and later, those of the road users.

Rex kept the heavy plant going at top performance by his regular daily maintenance. Large-scale mechanical troubles cropping up from time to time added considerably to his work. Gearboxes, transmissions, main bearings, and every conceivable mishap came his way constantly and were taken care of promptly and efficiently. Even when his conscience told him he should not be away from his family for such long periods and he reluctantly left the Gunbarrel Road Construction Party, he still played a major role later in the project.

Scotty, who was alone so long on the grader he thought "Grader Garbo" would be a more suitable name, had already graded well over 3000 kilometres of our roads involving some 24 400 kilometres of actual grading. His belt-line had moulded to the shape of the machine's steering wheel which he held with a firm pressure of his stomach while his hands worked the array of six wheel and blade control levers spaced on either side of the centre-line. His task was lightened a little by Doug's practised hand on the bulldozer blade lift winch. He had also been with us from the beginning. His final straight cuts from the dozer blade left behind a road easy to drive on, a smooth, endless ribbon of cleared surface quite unlike the mountains and great holes I'd leave after my occasional efforts on his machine.

The exact spot where we were all assembled had been chosen after a number of bush reconnaissance surveys I had made while trying to find an access from the south side of the Rawlinson Range system to the north. The system extended unbroken for 110 kilometres roughly east to west with the one exception of a narrow pass sixteen kilometres from the eastern end. Then the Petermann Ranges began, going further east. As the narrow pass didn't lend itself very well to a northern route, the area between the two main systems had to be used. A waterway named "The Rebecca" by the explorer Ernest Giles in 1874 passed through the same gap and was the only obvious access to the north.

Our point of assembly was to become one of the main junctions in our Central Australian road system, situated alongside a small, shady stand of desert oaks on an otherwise bare spinifex flat. Thirty kilometres to the west of the junction lay the meteorological station named after Giles, the first white man to travel into this country on horses nearly eighty years before. We had established the station four years ago, to supply weather information to the scientists 1100 kilometres away at Maralinga, so that dates could be arrived at on which their atomic bombs could be safely detonated. Conditions in the upper atmosphere, which would carry the future radioactive fallout from the tests, would first be examined by the bureau staff at Giles and their findings transmitted to the atomic range. The bombs could then be fired by the team when they knew that the active dust would be transported to fall harmlessly in the Gibson Desert area.

Acting on Quinny's suggestion, Doug climbed up on to the dozer, started the engine, and drove it off the low-loader on to the sand, flattening spinifex clumps in the way. Paul lumbered his ration wagon over to the stand of desert oaks and began collecting some wood while Scotty and Rex serviced the grader, which was necessary after the long drive. The low-loader driver prepared the float for its

23

return to Adelaide, with the great weight of the dozer replaced by all the empty drums we had accumulated on the trip.

The bulldozer was ready for instant use, having been carried from the servicing workshop half-a-month's drive away. It was manoeuvred into a position across the existing road which I'd carefully planned after the survey, and its blade lowered in readiness. I drove off north along my reconnaissance tracks for one-and-a-half kilometres and flashed a mirror reflection of the sun back to Doug across the spinifex plain and was rewarded by an answering burst from the diesel. Three seconds later, yet another road junction had come into being as the blade wiped that section of the old windrow away and came towards me. It was the last day of March 1960, and the Central Australian summer sun was still beating down in full force, so that from my simmering Land Rover the big machine seemed to be a quivering, yellow, jellylike mass floating in the ground mirage.

We made one-and-a-half kilometres of road in what was left of the day, and leaving the machine at its head behind a mountain of spinifex, we returned to the camp at the brand-new junction in my Rover, to resume the work on April Fools' Day. Someone remarked how appropriate that was, for it was crazy being in this country at this time of the year in the first place. But seasons couldn't be allowed to interrupt our project, as we had a long, long way to go and the access roads were needed for the overall programme at Woomera.

This was the first trip that our small camp included a caravan. It was suggested by the party so at least two or three members could sleep out of the elements for a change, as we'd been sleeping in the open for many years. The very popular superintendent of Woomera at the time, Colonel Durance, was overwhelming in his offers of any caravan I wanted out of the dozens grouped for accommodating overflows of scientists who commuted in force from Salisbury during rocket trials. The grader would be able to tow it anywhere, and at a pinch the bulldozer

24

would either get it over any of the very bad sandhills we were sure to encounter, or pull it in half trying. I made an inspection of them all and chose a small one which the workshops modified so that it could be towed behind anything we had. The dressing-table was dispensed with for we had nothing to put on top of it, but the shiny wardrobe might come in handy to put in raggy pairs of shorts and overalls dripping with dieseline, so it was left. Doug, Scotty, and Eric had thought of the idea and would be the ones to use it, while Quinny and Rex would resume their bedrooms on the built-in 300-gallon water tanks adjoining the 100-gallon petrol tanks in the back of their trucks. Paul liked the open air beside his ration truck and wouldn't want to change.

I lived beside my Rover in the open. I had to be self-contained at all times because I spent a great deal of the time on my own exploring ahead of the road for the route that the future access would follow. While in the camp guiding the dozer, I had afforded myself the extreme luxury of an iron and wire hospital-type bed, with a thin covering so the crisscross wire top wouldn't be left imprinted on my back. This would be hung on the side of the Rover on two iron hooks I had made with forge and anvil in a blacksmith's shop and a leather strap stopped the bottom from flapping against the mudguard. The bed was part of the vehicle except on long expeditions when the mulga scrub constantly tearing along the sides of the Rover would rake all the wire out of it. Before leaving the camp for such a trip I would set it up under a tree, heap any surplus gear on it, and cover it with a roped-down canvas camp-sheet. Then I would revert to sleeping on a square of canvas on the ground, as I had done for so many years before. This would also leave more room for tins of petrol on the vehicle and keep the things I'd left behind off the ground away from the white ants. Even that didn't help all the time. I returned once to find that in only a fortnight the termites had built a miniature castle high enough to reach a spare pair of hobnailed boots and had completely eaten the sides out of them.

Whenever I passed through the last cattle station on our way to the desert, the iron frame with its wire netting stretched across it was always hanging on the side of my Rover. One little boy there, who had seen it each time, asked why on earth I was forever carrying a gate about with me.

In three days' time we had progressed as far as a dry watercourse which the explorer Ernest Giles discovered in 1874 and named after himself. My road necessarily had to cross over its loose sandy bed at right angles so we moved our camp from the junction to its banks. We worked on it for a day with chopped logs mixed with dirt bulldozed from the harder ground. A good rain could start the water flowing temporarily and wash the road away but in this arid area it might be many years before this occurred. By then the main use would have been made of the crossing anyway. As it happened, I drove over it ten years later and found it was still quite passable without becoming sand-bogged.

A group of Aborigines whom we had first met in this country years before and who were still good friends with us, appeared near our camp while we were working on the Giles Creek crossing. They had been attracted by the commotion made by the big diesels and remained hovering about for weeks, following the camp as we moved. One day I was ahead on my own sorting out where to locate the road through a confused area of rock outcrops near the western end of the Kathleen Range. I was concentrating on slowly forcing the Rover through the thickest stand of dry mulgas I had encountered so far. The operation of guiding the wheels past possible mulga stakes, which sometimes insisted on flattening my tyres at the rate of six a day, was taking all my attention, with the only sound in the quiet bush that of the branches raking along the sides. Suddenly a high-pitched voice from nowhere yelled out a greeting which all but made me collapse with fright at the wheel. Yowina, a little Aboriginal boy I had known since he was not much older than a baby, was gesturing excitedly outside the closed perspex window. He

26

laughed until he fell down to the ground at the obvious shock he had caused me. The Land Rover stopped dead against a wall of mulga by the simple action of using the clutch, and it took some performance to push the door open through the branches. The little black body, completely naked in the heat of the day, was still rolling about in the dirt with delighted shrieks of mirth, and when he finally stood up his sweaty skin had mopped up the red dust till he had taken on a shade a half-a-dozen times paler than usual. He was very ready to accept a tin mug of water from my tank and we travelled together for the rest of the day, with him walking alongside easily keeping up.

The Kathleen Range forms a sort of trailing-off finish to the western extremity of the Petermann Ranges. After clearing this I had to ease the course of the road over in such a way as to clear the eastern end of the Schwerin Mural Crescent which was in turn a similar extension of the eastern terminus of the Rawlinson Range. I had planned all this from a separate reconnaissance which governed the actual location of the new junction.

Nearly five years before we had put down bores to supply the Giles weather station with water. Now some small surveys were needed of their various levels, with an eye to ordering engines and pumps of the correct capacity to push the water up to the station. This we did before starting on the new road. We spent a pleasant few days there with the plentiful water showers and good food laid on. On the job in the bush the heat and mists of black flies were the same as usual, but the evenings at Giles could be looked forward to as a welcome spell from nights in the scrub with very limited water and no escape from the flies. At least the flies eased up their feverish activities after sundown but the ovenlike heat sometimes lasted all night long.

As the weather station became more established they even set up film shows. We'd lie about in the open while anyone who could operate the projector shone the films on to a white-painted board nailed to the ablutions shed wall. The projector was powered by the same generator we had towed behind a truck 1600 kilometres to the site, and which provided current for the radar used to track the radio sondes attached to meteorological balloons.

One night some Aborigines crept up from their camp on the mulga-lined banks of the Sladen Waters creek, whose dry course lay between the Rawlinson Range and the weather station huts. The film on this particular evening showed a well-known actress landing a huge passenger airliner on her own with the pilots dead or dying all around her. An exceptionally large and unusually fat Aboriginal made up part of the audience. When the critical point arrived as the plane screamed down on an erratic approach to the runway, our huge friend was sweating, shaking, and holding his hands over his face, with the whites of his eyes only showing through slits between his fingers. Although the drama being enacted on the wash-house wall was one of the most tense one could hope to see, we were watching the antics of the Aboriginal and listening to his yells of fright in his anticipation of the imminent disaster about to take place. He really thought he was on that plane descending on the San Francisco airport and was sure his life on this earth was limited to the next three microseconds. I think all of us missed the actual crash down as the tyres screamed on the tarmac, but one glance at the airport lights and buildings rocketing past the cockpit was enough to assure us that the aircraft with its passengers was still intact and we returned our attention to the fearful watcher. His shrieks and actions told us what was going on as he weaved and ducked when another post or building was narrowly missed by the girl at the controls. By the time she had brought the machine to a halt at right angles to the strip, we were laughing so hard at our visitor the tears were streaming down our faces. A second later the film ran out and the loose end flapped against the empty spool as it spun, causing a loud slapping noise which made the man jump up with surprising agility for his size and head off through the mulga for his camp. He'd had enough of picture shows to last him for the rest of his life.

Although we liked to make our roads straight where

28

possible, the intervening country between Giles Creek and the pass at the end of the Mural Crescent was dotted with some beautiful stands of desert oaks, and rather than damage them we veered the road to left and right, leaving the stately trunks virtually lining the bulldozed cut. It was a most pleasant area and I couldn't bring myself to disfigure it any more than was necessary for our work. At one dry creek-crossing which had to be made I found a most spectacular white ghost gum on the opposite bank and that governed where the future road would be at that point. Now as people drive down and over the steep banks, cut back to form a ramp, they pass beside the white trunk in the shade cast by the bright green foliage. A sort of private road beautification scheme, even out there in the desert.

The sight of one straight desert oak trunk we had been forced to reluctantly bulldoze down brought to mind the need for one of the usual signposts we would always erect at any junction or fork in the roads for the use and safety of future travellers. I chopped off a three-metre length and squared one end with my razor-sharp survey axe, then capped the end with sheet lead brought for the purpose. The actual sign was made from a rectangular aluminium plate also specially carried. This involved sitting down for an hour in the sand between the spinifex with the aluminium on a heavy jack plate, while I stamped out the message with a hammer and letter punches. The wording included the observed latitude and longitude value; the distances either way to the next feature on the road, sometimes up to 1600 kilometres off; the date; and often the names of the members of the little camp and their function with us. I would always add a line pointing out that the "road was made by the Gunbarrel Road Construction Party" so future travellers would know who to blame. I often felt this was much like the Egyptians carrying out ancient writings letter by letter on a rock slab thousands of years ago; in the same period hence, who knows but our signs may be guarded behind glass in a museum.

When finished, this was nailed to the squared end of the

29

tree trunk with galvanised brads, and the whole thing carried on the bonnet of the Rover to the site of our recent new junction. After digging with crowbar and shovel, the post was eased into the hole and rammed solid while held upright by a helper. Where possible we would save old, staked truck and Rover tyres, or even useless grader tyres for such occasions, and place these in order of size around the base, centred over the post. The spaces were filled with dirt or rocks. Resembling a giant game of deck quoits, this structure helped the sign's preservation. The whole thing, including the tyres, was then painted white and left for the people who would eventually make use of it. At that stage I thought it would be lucky to be six a year, but as the roads became established and appeared on maps I was amazed to discover just how many people for various reasons did actually travel on them.

Day by day as I surveyed the exact route ahead of the bulldozer I would leave the iron bed back in the camp to save it from being raked to pieces by the mulga branches. One afternoon I returned to camp to find little Yowina lying on its bare fence-pattern wire, sound asleep. He was completely naked as always and when I drove alongside, I managed to photograph him before he woke. Soon he opened his eyes and stretched, disturbing the black mist of flies which afforded him some shade from the still-blazing sun, and swung his legs to the ground. As he walked back to his own camp a little distance off, I wondered how long you would be able to play chess on his bare back using the deeply-imprinted squared pattern clearly left by the bed.

4

Before We Called
it Woomera

It would be quite justifiable to say that this whole operation stemmed from the inception of the Woomera Rocket Range and the need for large-scale surveys for the tracking instrumentation involved. That, coupled with the requirements for the atomic ranges, provided the reasons for opening up vast, untouched areas of Central and Western Australia. The first inkling that such a range was being thought of came to me in a casual remark made by the then Director of the Australian Army Survey Corps, Colonel Fitzgerald, as we leant against a mantelpiece over an old fireplace in the Melbourne Observatory buildings.

I had just driven in after accompanying a scientific expedition with a combination of experts in various fields from the CSIRO in Canberra, which had spent almost a year in the Alligator River country of the Northern Territory's Arnhem Land. I had gone along in 1946 in response to a request to the army for someone to carry out astronomical observations for the small expedition, so that their scientific discoveries and results could be recorded in map form.

31

While I was yarning to the Colonel about the year's work, he mentioned that the Corps had just been approached by a small team of Englishmen who had asked if it would be possible for us to send somebody over to South Australia to start "some sort of a rocket range— er—or something". Apparently towards the close of the second World War, it became necessary to develop and test missiles of various types. Six scientists in England were selected to look into the prospect of locating a suitable site somewhere in the British Empire large enough to conduct the trials as the projectiles were developed. We both knew that this or any other similar undertaking in remote areas would involve an enormous number of star observations and associated calculations for pinpointing positions and bearings on the surface of the earth, and I seemed to be a reasonable sort of choice. Of course this was quite apart from the fact that members of the Corps were obtaining their discharges from the army at a great rate after service in a long war, and there weren't many left to choose from. So when I was asked if I would be willing to remain in the army for another year, it was a turning point in my life which was to govern the next quarter of a century.

The colonel went on to tell me, after I'd agreed to waive my discharge rights for another year, that when I got to Adelaide I was to contact an English general there who was in charge of the team, and find out what it was all about.

His name was General Evetts, and he was later knighted for his work and became General Sir John Evetts. British army officers of that rank were people I hadn't had very much to do with. Before leaving Melbourne our own director realised this and sent me off to Victoria Barracks to obtain a more conventional Australian army uniform. It replaced my shorts worn under a battle-dress jacket held together by a standard Japanese army issue belt I'd acquired in one of their camps in the jungle near Wewak in New Guinea. The fact that the original owner had no more use for it would have made it seem otherwise a waste.

The regimental sergeant-major at the barracks couldn't

believe his eyes when I ambled into the guard post in my regalia, including a huge pair of hobnailed boots and army-type "half-hose" pulled up. The expanse of bare ankle between the two had, I decided, to be covered up, which I accomplished by wrapping a canvas gaiter around each leg. I didn't have a slouch hat, the one I had been issued with having been trampled by a buffalo in Arnhem Land during the year, but the first thing the astounded R.S.M. spluttered about was the belt. I pointed out I had to wear it to hold my watch and penknife pouches, as after all I'd just got in from the bush. In the C.O.'s office, where he had hustled me quickly to prevent as many soldiers as possible from seeing me, I was shown a despatch which had been sent in advance as a warning. It read that our unit would be grateful if they could re-outfit a bush-ranger who would arrive on their doorstep shortly wearing a hunting knife on his belt. They added that I was in fact a soldier in the same army but any resemblance was purely coincidental.

In no time I was sitting on the C.O.'s glass-topped desk, sketching crocodiles and Aborigines with whom I had very recently been in contact, on his blotting pad, and generally giving him and the poor R.S.M., still rigidly standing to attention, a travel talk about the much-publicised scientific expedition into the remote parts of the Alligator and Wildman river country. After several hours, during which other officers had gathered to form a sizeable audience, even the R.S.M. thawed and the C.O. seemed reluctant to send me off to the quartermaster to get into a more conventional costume. He almost apologised by pointing out that it was the army after all, and the military police did have a thankless job to do.

When I returned to the observatory I was shown a second reply despatch stating that the bushranger had been taken care of and pointing out that the job of endeavouring to tame him was now up to them. A foot-note from the C.O. of one of the strictest and most regi-mented barracks in Australia mentioned that they had a job on their hands which he secretly hoped they wouldn't accomplish. I deduced from this that he was human after all.

Armed with my new hat complete with shiny chin-strap and puggaree, a matching uniform, boots laced up in a parallel pattern as against my crisscross method, socks with feet in them, and regulation webbing belt, I set off for Adelaide to start "some sort of a rocket range or something". The slight bulges in the service-dress jacket were made by the watch and penknife pouches still attached to the Japanese belt, but now worn underneath and out of sight.

I was met in Adelaide by a green-and-yellow camouflaged army jeep from Keswick Barracks and transported through the city to the South Australian counterpart of the grey rock establishment with which I had so recently been entangled in Victoria. I could feel that sense of trepidation, as though they were wondering just what to expect, having been forewarned of my arrival. This eased when they saw I was, if only temporarily, normal in outward appearance anyway. They confided they had been expecting Ned Kelly in person at least and in fact I had to reveal the bulge in my jacket to convince them it was not really made by a holstered revolver.

Major Lindsay Lockwood from our Survey Corps was already installed in the barracks to coordinate these activities and we got together immediately, much to the relief of the C.O., glad to have me off his hands. I thought that if this kept up, I would be getting a complex.

The visit to interview the British general came next, and on the way through the main streets of Adelaide in a canvas-topped army jeep given to me for the purpose, I was stopped in a line of heavy traffic by a policeman. There were cars everywhere and while waiting for him to sort out the crush, I casually glanced around behind me after hearing a peculiar noise. There, occupying the rear compartment, was the head of a horse, winkers and all, regarding me balefully with tired, big, brown eyes, as a globule of white foam dripped from the end of the bit in his mouth on to the back seat. On looking further I

Top: I discovered the unknown tribe of Aborigines soon after I had found water in this creek, which I later named "Lolly Water". *Bottom:* Evidence of the tribe. This line of stones, 100 metres long and running exactly north and south, was far removed from the nearest rock outcrop

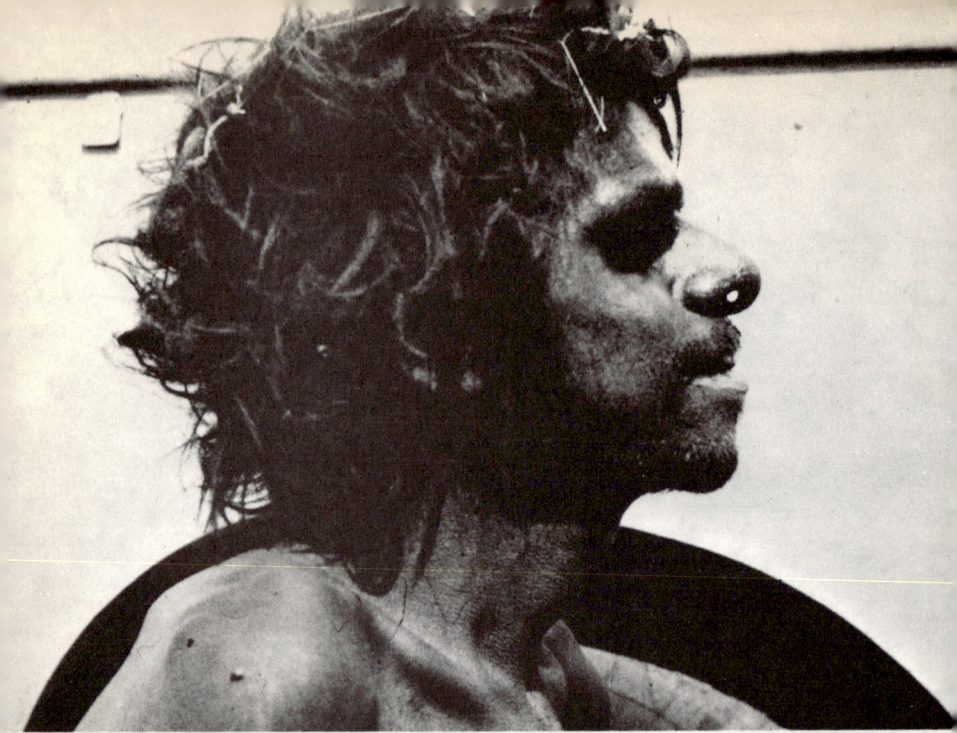

noticed he was still harnessed to a cart which had not stopped as soon as I did, leaving the unfortunate horse with no alternative but to thread his head through the vertical opening in the canvas hood. By then the man from the force was waving us on, but we all had to pool our resources to extricate the head while at the same time leaving the ears which had sprung upright after the squeeze, still attached to the head.

I was sure that this could only happen to me and I couldn't wait to get back to the bush where I seemed to belong.

Eventually, with the jeep parked, probably illegally, outside the general's hotel, I was waiting for him in the lobby after the receptionist had called him. The tall, ramrod-straight officer with the toothbrush moustache approached, and I made myself known to him. He was slightly built and although he wore glasses, a monocle would have looked quite in place, I thought. He started straight in with the observation that they would need quite a large area for this rocket range, "eh what?" After I told him I knew of 2.6 million square kilometres of virtually unexplored sandhills and spinifex country in Central and Western Australia, he exclaimed, "By Jove, that's much more than we've got in Gloucester!" The birth of the rocket range was on the way there and then, although at the time I thought it was only going to be a one-night fireworks display akin to the Guy Fawkes exhibition, and didn't dream it would develop into a "village" of 7000 people.

Later, after several air reconnaissance flights, an area 160 kilometres north-west of Port Augusta seemed to be roomy enough for development. Also an extensive flood in 1946, caused by a twenty-five-year cycle of torrential rains, had filled several usually dust-dry lakes to the brim. The country with a normal annual rainfall of 120 to 150 millimetres was deluged, leaving the few sheep station homesteads either on islands surrounded by horizons of rainwater, or partly submerged with the waves swirling half a metre deep around their pianos, as I was soon to find out.

Top: This Aboriginal had never seen a white man before. His septum had been pierced with a sharp stick or bone. *Bottom:* These attractive ghost gums between Mural Crescent and the Petermann Ranges led us to indulge in a private road beautification scheme

The sight of these freshwater lakes complete with swans and ducks made the area look like a veritable paradise; the water could be used to start our project immediately. I was told that the distance from the nearest town, Port Augusta, would be sufficient to allow any stray, off-course missiles to be destroyed in mid-air by radio before endangering any civilisation. Also only half a dozen stations lay between there and the Indian Ocean nearly 2400 kilometres to the north-west, and even these stopped within the first 300 kilometres. It was a perfect geographical location and an intensive survey of the area was first on the programme.

General Evetts' party consisted of a scientist, an engineer who had come to write reports of the progress to relay back to the British Government, and several other experts in the fields of rocketry and electronics.

In the jeep again, which I discovered had been left unmolested by parking inspectors, I drove back to the barracks to make a start on the stores of survey and camping equipment we would need. Other members of our first little survey party numbering about six in all were made available and the onslaught on the facilities of Keswick Barracks began. High on the list came poles and discs for the trig survey beacons as they were the first stage in laying down a triangulation network over the entire area, and I spent quite a time in the workshops to see they were made to our requirements—probably too much time for the peace of mind of the sheet-metal workers and other army tradesmen.

Vehicles needed modifying to cope with the job in hand. Racks to carry water and petrol and a truck to transport the bulk of our equipment gave the motor transport boys plenty to do as we planned what we needed. At this stage four jeeps and one three-ton truck comprised our whole outfit.

An extraordinary coincidence occurred on another visit to Adelaide to select some items for star observation which were not usually to be found in army stores. I stopped again in heavy traffic, heard a noise behind me, turned around, and said to no one in particular "Here we go again". The open back window of my jeep seemed to hold some sort of morbid fascination for horses, I thought, as I pushed one ear after the other back out through the hole, followed closely by the winkers.

Knowing just what amount of work lay ahead, we were as anxious as General Evetts and his party to get on with it. In a relatively short time we drove our five vehicles, loaded with trig poles, theodolites, and porridge, out of the gates of the barracks bound for a site as yet unknown in detail, 480 kilometres distant. We were on our way at last.

While at Port Augusta the party seemed to have some vague idea that this was to be their last sight of civilisation for some time to come, and indicated they would like to stay overnight and continue in the morning. It was late afternoon so I set out alone to drive the slow three-ton truck until dark, after arranging for them to follow in the four jeeps the next day. At that stage there was only one road in the direction we were going: just well-used wheel-tracks through the saltbush and mulga, which had originally been made and used in the latter part of the last century by a horse team and coach. This travelled about 300 kilometres to Kingoonya, now a siding on the main east-west railway, bringing mail and passengers to the various sheep stations on the way which were then in their early stages of development. The horse team was changed half-way at a place named Phillip Ponds which was where we were bound for, as it was quite centrally situated near the fresh lakes and only ten kilometres from the railway siding at Pimba. The teams were watered on the way at underground concrete tanks covered by roofing iron and placed in positions where they could best be filled by the scant rainwater which would trickle down the natural folds in the topography. The roofs were also used as catchment to channel water into the tank. A horse trough and pump completed these watering stops and made it possible for the Royal Mail to get through.

After I drove the truck slowly out of Port Augusta, it was to be ten months before I saw another glimpse of a settlement. As I cleared the last few houses in a kilometre or so, the saltbush took over. It was all I would see for nearly a year. I noticed black clouds building up in the sky followed by a few spots of rain which made me glad I had decided to head off when I did. The lighter jeeps could pull each other out of bogs but the heavy army blitz truck was another story, so I endeavoured to get as far as possible before camping.

After eighty kilometres the wheeltracks passed a lonely grave with a marble headstone, surrounded by a broken fence. Here some early traveller had been laid to rest. By then the rain was pouring down so I didn't climb out to read the inscription. A couple of hundred metres beyond that, the headlights picked out a stony patch off the road on a slightly raised level and as it had been black night for several hours already, I decided to stop and camp. With the truck on the higher ground, it wouldn't sink into a bog during the rest of the night at least, and I could survey the situation in daylight to see if it were safe to drive down on to the track or if I should wait until things dried out. There was ample room under the vehicle out of the rain so I rolled out my swag between the back wheels and lay down.

The night was inky black, broken by forks of lightning. The rain poured down incessantly and kept me awake lying there on the stones for at least an hour, overtired as I was. Then around midnight I suddenly heard an engine revving back along the road in the direction of the grave. It kept up for half an hour as though someone was trying to extract a motor car from a bog but getting in deeper with every wheel-spinning revolution of his engine. I thought about the lonely headstone, glowing white with each flash of lightning, the only witness to this episode being enacted close by at midnight, and it all sounded quite eerie. I could not do much with the lorry and had no idea, but for the sound and direction, how far away he was. Apart from sitting up and probing the blackness from under the truck for his lights, I stayed where I was, determining to help him when morning came. Eventually the sounds stopped and, as I hadn't been able to see any evidence of headlights through the rain-soaked mulga scrub, I finally went to sleep after the bruise I'd collected on my forehead, by hitting it on the steel tail-shaft when I sat up, had stopped throbbing.

Next morning the rain had gone but the country was a sea of red mud, so I began walking back between the twin rivulets of water forming in the wheeltracks in search of my as yet unseen midnight neighbour. I reached the gravestone and kept on for a kilometre but not a sign or trace of a bogged vehicle or fresh mud tracks could I see. A little further on I emerged from the mulga patch to see the old tracks stretching away across open saltbush flats but still not a suggestion of anything else.

As I plodded back in my mud-clogged boots, I relived the happenings of that night and the sure feeling I had had of finding a lone bushman in trouble within very easy walking distance of my gloomy camp. I could ask the boys when I saw them later if they had been anything on their way to me in the jeeps, but right then, as I dragged my boots one after the other through the mud past the tombstone gleaming in the morning sunlight, I felt a sense of weirdness I wanted to explain away. When the rest of the party eventually turned up, none of them had seen a thing since leaving Port Augusta. The final answer to it all has never been found.

When I tried to press on, I discovered that although the wheeltracks were miniature creeks, they had been compacted enough over the years to be able to support my truck. Still thinking about the unexplained drama, I sloshed the tyre-slackened truck away from the scene. Every time I have driven past the spot in the succeeding quarter of a century I can't help but bring to mind the ghostly unaccountable noises by the old white tombstone in the bush. The stone is still there today as good as ever but is rarely seen by travellers owing to the subsequent relocation of the main road to Woomera, bypassing the spot several hundred metres away.

By mid-afternoon the faster jeeps had all caught up to my lumbering wagon and we pulled up for something to eat. The area was so bare that someone remarked that "you could see a bull-ant for ten miles in any direction." According to the only map we could find of the area we had about thirty kilometres to go to reach Phillip Ponds. We planned to have the jeeps continue on to give the cook time to settle in before nightfall and get something on for tea, while I would grind on slowly behind.

We were making for an old stone outstation which had been used originally as a coach-house about seventy years before. Later it was occupied by old Joe Stanford and his family who moved about that country working for various stations as the jobs came to hand. It had been empty for the previous ten years, and we planned to use it for survey instrument storage, and for calculations and plotting of fieldwork. We would also use one room for meals at the odd times when we returned to this base from temporary survey camps in a radius of about eighty kilometres.

The outstation belonged to the Arcoona sheep station which spread for nearly 4000 square kilometres over the area to be studied for future testing of rockets. We had contacted the owners and discovered that a stone and cement rainwater tank lay underground next to the building and was still full of water from the previous year's floods. There was also a stove and from the appearance of the surrounding country, we would need to carry the wood for it quite a distance.

Eventually the pattern of the country changed, and from the crest of a hill I looked over the intervening small watercourse to see the roof of the old stone coach-house. Smoke was already coming from the chimney, indicating that Joe Fitzgerald, our first cook, was getting on with his job. The sight of it made me remember that apart from the piece of bread and jam I'd had when we all met recently, I hadn't eaten anything since leaving Port Augusta the previous afternoon.

Quite eagerly I headed the blitz down the stony incline

40

and started out along the flat at the bottom to cover the last 300 metres to my future home. No sooner had the truck progressed a few metres along the flat, than I was shaken by the sound of a loud explosion at the rear. Just as I was thinking that it was a bit soon for the rocket trials to be taking place, the truck dropped down at the offside back corner and I knew the big tyre had collapsed. Within a couple of minutes' walk of the destination, I was forced to unload the jack and tools and begin to repair the first of a long line of mishaps which beset this project.

The boys noticed that the truck seemed a long time in closing the remaining distance to "the Ponds" as we ever after referred to this camp, so they jumped into a jeep and came over. I could hear their laughter a hundred metres away before they reached me.

After putting up a couple of tents outside the house on the stony, quartzite saltbush flat, we felt at last that this huge programme was really under way. The date was Wednesday 12 March 1947.

5

"Home on the Range"

At first light next morning Lindsay Lockwood and I headed across the bare tableland in an open jeep towards a slight rise, referred to as "Pearson's Hill" in an original old survey field book which I had examined at the Lands Office in Adelaide before leaving. An early triangulation had been carried out in this very area by surveyor Joseph Brooks from June 1875 to November 1876. His huge field book of the results was a work of art. Containing not only the actual numerical entries, it was also embellished with the most beautiful water-colour paintings of scenes around the trig hills. His mulga trees and views would enable others to relocate his survey marks, for each picture was equivalent to a colour photograph of the locality, neatly framed in interlocking geometrical figures of hexagons, triangles, circles, and ovals. Every page was different.

Pearson's Hill was located within ten kilometres of the Ponds. By the simple procedure of making for the higher ground in that general area, we were bound to come to it. Driving across the expanse of gibbers and saltbush presented no problems at all and eventually, as the country rose, an uninterrupted skyline presented itself as far as the eye could see all around us. There was no wood for trig poles at these old triangulation stations so stone cairns had been built using material gathered from the surface. The highest point in the surrounding country is always selected for trig stations to give the maximum visibility both away from and back to the point, but in this case anywhere for hundreds of metres could have been chosen.

As one could "see a bull-ant for ten miles" in this country, the mound of quartzite was easy to detect from a distance and we soon began pulling it down to reach the ground mark which is the main point of a trig station. All angles, distances, and values are referred to the survey mark itself and the above-ground cairn or pole is merely a beacon to be sighted from other trigs. In this case the cairn could once have supported a wooden post carried by camel wagon for many kilometres for the job, but no sign of it remained, and the once neat, sizeable monument of stones was now just an unshapely heap. Quartzite, of metamorphosed sedimentary origin, is hard and smooth, and won't grip together as rougher or softer rocks do. If the lower ones slip off each other, the whole pile is reduced to rubble in seconds. By carefully placing the stones to prevent this, the old surveyors had been successful in leaving some of the many cairns we were to find during the subsequent months in almost their original shape. More often than not, we found them in a state like this first one at Pearson's Hill.

As we removed the stones we came upon various types of little creatures which had been living among them. One of the more interesting was a barking lizard who wasn't at all impressed at the way we were manhandling his ancestral home. About ten centimetres long with little arms complete with elbows, and fingers on his hands, he (or she) raised himself up and coughed at us aggressively with his head cocked on one side to clearly indicate disenchantment at the proceedings. The two huge eyes, which together were as large as the rest of the head, glared at us, while the swollen plumb-bob-shaped tail fell away at

43

the other end, as is usual with some kinds of geckos. I made a quick pencil sketch of him in my field book and looked him up later as I hadn't seen the species before. I discovered it was a *Gymnodactylus milii* which means, as we noticed, that it has naked fingers or toes. The book even referred to its vertical eye slits and translucency of body where some bones and veins could be seen under the thin skin.

Eventually we reached the ground level at the centre of the dismantled mound and, sure enough, there was a larger flat slab of quartzite sunk a little way into the red laterite dirt. A circle complete with two diameters of ten centimetres crossing at right angles had been chipped into the smooth surface, with a small image of a broad arrow included in one of the quadrants. Looking at it in awed silence, we both knew that nobody, black or white, would have laid eyes on it since Joseph Brooks had placed it there over seventy years ago. We could re-enact the scene in our mind's eye: the old bush surveyor, probably moustached and bearded, in long worn trousers, hobnailed boots, and waistcoat, standing there at his unenamelled brass theodolite, reading the silver vernier scales and entering the figures in that big field book. Then he would have returned his attention to the instrument on its solid cedar tripod with the shiny brass plumb-bob hanging accurately over the intersection of the diameters on the stone slab, and aimed the telescope at the next trig beacon in his round of angles. One brown hand would feel for the external focusing screw as his gaze moved to the eyepiece, while the other would turn the brass clamp, bright with constant use. The next move would be to carefully intersect the distant trig beacon by slowly turning the equally bright tangent screw to move the spiderweb crosswires until they optically split the object down the middle, and once more the reading on the silver scale would have been noted.

So it was with reluctance that we placed two solid recovery marks and took up Brooks' relatively shallow ground mark. We dug a deep hole, filled it with the concrete we had mixed, and smoothed it off around an iron spike driven deeply into the middle which we relined by means of the recovery marks to precisely coincide with the lateral position of the original. Having finished, we sat on opposite sides of our handiwork and observed that it had at last started; "it" meaning what has grown finally into the huge complex of the Australian-based rocket range named Woomera. The permanent survey mark on Pearson's Hill was the first positive, on-site step to be taken, and still none of us dreamed in our wildest imagination just what it was we were starting.

Alongside the wet cement we temporarily put up one of the iron trig poles carried on the mudguard of the jeep. When the cement had set we would return to plumb the pole accurately over the mark. We drove back across the shimmering hot tableland to our camp. The Ponds dam, a basin scraped out of the ground a hundred metres from the old homestead, was still full of water, although it was a perfect example of a colloidal suspension of clay which made it impossible to see further than a fraction below the surface. On arrival we dived into it, shorts and all (minus belt, and watch and penknife pouches), carrying out two operations at once: our own bathing and the week's washing as well.

The green feed brought on by the flood had in turn made the rabbits healthy and happy and they were present in thousands, eating the saltbush within metres of our camp every night. In places their numbers made the ground seem to move. Usually driving back to camp well after dark, our strong little headlights would sweep over a furry carpet of bodies all intent on being somewhere else as the light shone on them. In the succeeding years we never found the plague repeated. Even mosquitoes were present in black clouds every night, making late afternoon angle observing most difficult; when one hand was brushed down the opposite forearm it would leave a wide black road of smeared bodies. These were days which later workers at Woomera could not believe ever happened; flies certainly, but mosquitoes and rabbits in those proportions, never. Foxes thrived on the rabbits, and eagles

45

and crows ate the foxes; black swans floated gracefully on the surface of the numerous freshwater lakes. Kangaroos moved about in hordes and one could lose count after reaching several dozen. I didn't know how rare an occurrence all this was, so I constantly wondered why people hadn't long ago flocked to this paradise of a place to lead an ideal Shangri-la type of existence by the lakesides.

The original survey party was made up of a wonderful little group from the army survey corps who all worked well together, helping each other between their own jobs, and were constantly agreeable, with a spontaneous sense of humour. Frank Cohen and I had spent the previous year together in the Alligator River country of the Northern Territory so we were just continuing our long rough spell in the bush. Frank was therefore well used to computing survey results and the two of us would be able to re-check the calculations involved in the urgently-required astronomical observations on this job. Harold Watts, a tall, dark member of the party, originally came from the country. Apart from setting rabbit traps every night as a sideline, he was also practised at the various tasks in surveying we needed to start a rocket range.

Then came Johnny Showers from the mountain country of northern Victoria and he also was a technical instrument operator, later to be valuable as the only person who could verify my story that we both saw three rabbits sitting on the topmost branches of a scraggy, tall mulga tree, eating the foliage. Nobody but the oldest bushmen believes me when I insist that in a drought we did see three furry shapes high on mulga branches as we drove along in our jeep. We ventured closer and the three apparitions leapt from branch to branch down the trunks, revealing that they were not in fact koala bears but rabbits, which scurried into their respective burrows in a dusty warren. In droughts they have been known to learn to climb trees for feed but rarely has anyone actually seen them in the act. Consequently, I have always had to quote Johnny as my one reliable witness to show that I hadn't already been too long in the bush.

With his red hair and white skin, Ivan Millar had the most unfortunate complexion for the searing sun in this shadeless country, but he was so willing and capable it didn't seem to bother him at all. His favourite saying was "remorse"; his descriptions of particularly regretful incidents, always uttered in a low undertone, were either begun or finished with the word.

The next member of the group, although none of us knew it at the time, was to marry locally and a quarter of a century later he was still within 200 kilometres of our old camp at the Ponds. He was Bill Osborne or Ozzie, so natural a nickname that no one ever used his real one. A wild jeep driver, he always drove his vehicle expertly at the greatest speed the terrain would allow, resulting in the bane of his life being broken springs, chassis shackles, and speedo cables. Everything happened to him, mostly not through his own fault. Someone would drive the truck for months then in the first few hundred metres he took it, a tyre would blow or the engine seize up. A horse which had been ridden 160 kilometres to take part in a bush gymkhana was ridden by Ozzie in one of the races, using the same saddle. Halfway through the event the girth strap broke and deposited Ozzie, still sitting in the saddle, on the track, enveloped in powdery bulldust and narrowly missed by the hooves of the other horses.

Constantly misnamed Watermelon and Waterstone, Mick Waterland, a driver, was the shortest of the bunch at just over 130 centimetres tall, but he was also the oldest member. His teeth, usually worn in his pocket, made it hard for him to whistle, and as he didn't sing or talk much, most of the time we didn't know if he was still with us. He was the nicest person to be with in a hopelessly-bogged vehicle, for he would quietly set about extracting it, every movement planned and unhurried. We were all in our very early twenties and he was way up around the forty mark, almost senile, or so it seemed to us.

From the tall timber country in Victoria, and accordingly an expert axeman, Max Pickering, also an army driver,

47

often related stories of his bush boxing-ring bouts with friends in the timber camps and so he never seemed to be bothered by anyone. On this present job, his usefulness on the axe was to be wasted for quite some time as not a single tree appeared on the horizon and if one had, we wouldn't have touched it for anything. Even a stunted shrub, had there been one, would have assumed a value out of all proportion.

Every slice of camp-baked bread had to be of very precise and even thickness for Bill Fitzgerald, and a double loaf broken in the middle always had to be trimmed exactly before his piece could be cut. Bill was a survey assistant helping with whatever work came along. His namesake, Joe, made our gathering complete. Joe was the original cook who decided at an early stage that he would be more at ease back in the barracks cookhouse, but not before, and certainly not as a result of, the time he cooked a meal for General Evetts and his party who visited our camp later . . .

The general and his fellow top scientists were seated in the old Ponds homestead around our spotlessly-scrubbed wooden army table and, while waiting for their dinner, were discussing the project which was always uppermost in our thoughts. I happened to amble into the kitchen from outside, where I had been working on a jeep engine, when I heard a groan from Joe as he withdrew from the oven the plates laden with the best food we could find in our camp. He had been keeping the meals warm to be ready at a moment's notice when called for, but he was so anxious to present them still hot that he overdid the wood in the stove's firebox. Every dinner was burnt on the upper surface; the potatoes and meat were so black as to be impossible to serve, and he had nothing else to offer. I had a screwdriver still in my hand, a bit greasy but clean enough when wiped on my shorts, and to prevent Joe from bursting into tears I flicked each piece of food over to show the properly-cooked underside on top. As I did this, he cleaned off the gravy splashed on the edges of the plates with a towel and carried them in two at a time, returning for the next two which were given the screwdriver treatment in the meantime. I got him to take his time in placing them in front of our guests so that I could arrange the food in the most attractive way possible. Until the day he left our camp, Joe never failed to talk about the way the general applauded his wonderful cooking under such difficulties. I remembered returning to my jeep engine with gravy mixed with the grease wiped on my shorts.

Near by on a small, raised, flat spot on the gibbers outside the old homestead, stood a white marble headstone; a rectangular wrought-iron fence surrounding the grave had been erected over sixty years before, according to the inscription. The neat lettering explained that it was "Sacred to the memory of John Henry Davies, who died at Phillips Ponds on January 12, 1884 aged (about) 24 years". It went on to point out that this stone was erected by his fellow bushmen living at Mount Eba Station. I was to meet an oldtimer in the bush who actually knew John Henry and he retold the story which lay behind his death. Old Mick Kelly, as he was named, had subscribed to the cost of the stone. We talked while sitting on a log, and he pointed a gnarled, bent finger vaguely in the direction of the Ponds 100 kilometres away. He told me he knew what put Davies there: "Whisky put him there alright."

It wasn't long before Joe was replaced as cook by old George Greenwood. For two years in the bush he fed us with meals that could have been served in the most lavish eating place in any city. He was an absolute artist in his culinary ability and by far the most outstanding cook in my whole bush experience. Not only would he bake the most perfect loaves of fresh bread, but would somehow cultivate his own yeast out of potato peelings for the job. In the interim between Joe leaving and us finding another cook, various members of the party were rostered to take on the unenviable task and we lived on good plain food for weeks. There was nothing wrong with slabs of bully beef and tomato sauce with two-toned black and white scones, a billy of tea, and marmalade. One day we had a jelly which we drank, another a custard which was eaten with

49

knife and fork, and, as a refreshing change one morning, some porridge which stretched in an unbroken line from the billy to the tin plate when dished out. When the required length was reached we used a pair of tin shears to snip it off, allowing each end to spring back to its respective mound. After we pulled the ant-stopper stick from the hole punched in the top of the tin, we pumped milk on to the porridge by using a thumb on the bottom of the tin in an oil-can action. The sugar was wonderful. One of the braver impromptu cooks tried his hand at a sponge cake mix with dehydrated egg powder, but not being sure how long to leave it in the oven, he finished up frying lumps of it, and we ate it on toasted damper with Worcestershire sauce. It proved to be a most useful recipe which we were to use quite often, boiling it for scrambled eggs, adding flour and sugar for cakes, and replacing the sugar with diced carrots for Yorkshire pudding in stews.

Then came a telegraph message over the line at the Pimba railway siding to say that the general and his men would be paying us another visit, and Keswick Barracks asked if we could do with some temporary help during his stay. Although we were grateful to each other for our meals, we thought the more sensitive English stomachs might not be quite so used to our ways and perhaps a little assistance wouldn't go astray. Three men were subsequently loaned to us, who could put more time into looking after the nobility than we could, since we were so occupied with our work. We collected them at the siding from the west-bound train several days later. Not one of the three was under fifty-five years of age; dressed in their army uniforms complete with their first World War ribbons and with hats turned up at the sides, gaiters, and polished hobnailed boots, they looked an agreeable trio of old campaigners.

My first eager question was to ask if any of them could cook at all, and when I received three solemn head-shakes my heart sank to the level of my belted penknife pouch. I took them the ten kilometres across the saltbush flats to our camp and showed them their sleeping area and the

A member of the newly-found tribe. This man's conspicuous body markings were made by slashing the skin with a sharp stone and then filling in the cuts with ashes to produce weals. The mallee stick made handkerchiefs unnecessary

Ponds' dam open-air bathroom. It was early afternoon and Ivan's turn to cook the tea.

Soon the loud roaring of a motor coming from the direction of the Port Augusta road heralded the approach of a car which had quite obviously lost its muffler on the trip up, and which must be carrying the official party. We could see the vehicle leaning badly over to one side, indicating that it had also suffered bad spring breakages on the rough track, or that one of the members was of a particularly stout build. It coughed and spluttered past the spot where I had received my blowout in the truck not long before, and eventually the deafening roar of the open exhaust ceased as they stopped outside the homestead.

We invited the paleskins inside out of the blazing sun and Ivan had a billy of tea ready to offer the dusty, thirst-racked travellers. The general had bought a pair of shorts to wear since his last trip as a polite gesture towards the Australian boys in the bush, but they somehow seemed to look a little different on him. The bottom of the legs, almost sixty centimetres wide, came down to his knee-caps, and he had his long white socks pulled up almost touching them. I was slightly down the slope when he got out, so the six-millimetre strip of bare knee was at my eye-level, proving to me that the strange sight was in fact shorts, as broad as they were long, with two white legs emerging. The whole effect was not helped by the fact that they were made of red velvet.

Flat tyres are a continuing problem in the bush. Here I check the wheel of a Bristol Freighter before the Gunbarrel boys make a rare flight to Woomera

6

A Whirlwind Visit

Brigadier Barker had come to help the general with the military aspect, and Major Wynne-Williams from northern Wales was to write up the reports of the progress being made. These reports were dispatched to the British Government to keep it informed about this missile-testing site. Wynne, as he was usually called, arrived in what later became known as his standard rig-out. In the succeeding two years I never saw him wear anything other than his tweed jodhpurs with long woollen socks pulled up to his knees; except for the background of saltbush and gibbers, he looked like someone who'd come straight from an English hunt club. I was soon to discover that he had been left an enormous hole in a will; I wondered at the rather unusual bequest. The mystery was solved twelve years later when I visited him at his house near Caernarvon in northern Wales and he took me out, with a twinkle in his eye, to show me the hole he'd been left. It certainly proved huge; still in use, and vastly productive, it was one of the famous Welsh slate quarries.

Alan Butement, the man who was to become the chief

scientist in Australia for the whole project, was then introduced; it took me months to pronounce his name correctly and a year and a half to be able to spell it. From the very start he seemed to be the live-wire of the group and my first impressions of him didn't change during the following twenty-five years of our association. Within a minute he was eager to jump into my jeep for a ground tour of the area. His spirit infected the others and soon we were all charging out in a couple of jeeps over bare undulating country.

Always in a hurry, these people had to accomplish as much as possible in the shortest time, so at each stop, generally a survey mark I'd established which was also by design a good vantage point, volleys of questions were fired at me. Where to put a village; the direction of prevailing winds for an airfield orientation; how did the ground respond to wet-weather travel; what was the depth of the freshwater lakes for a possible water supply to start the project; whether or not the billions of mosquitoes were to be catered for in planning? On and on they came, until gradually I got the idea that perhaps this wasn't to be a one-night fireworks display after all, and might last up to a week.

Throughout the day I couldn't help thinking about what we were going to give this high-level group to eat for their tea when we at last returned to our Ponds camp. I wondered how they would react to scrambled, baked eggs and elastic porridge.

From the day's work I gathered I was to concentrate on locating an airfield site which would need the least amount of earthworks for its construction. I had to keep an eye out for the positioning of a village with respect to the approach funnel to the aerodrome. A landing field has specific conditions laid down for its approaches and no construction must take place within these bounds in case of possible aircraft mishaps either taking off or landing. Each site depended on the other, so it was going to be a difficult job, but it would be helped considerably by referring to the contour maps we had been drawing since our

53

arrival. To find two-and-a-half kilometres of quite level ground even in this bald country was not as easy as it first appeared.

At long last they had had enough and we pointed our radiators for home and tea, or so I hoped. I wasn't hoping so much that we were headed straight for our camp, as I could arrive there from any direction even at night; it was the meal I was worried about. We couldn't rely on a screwdriver to mend the food as before, but I was sure our impromptu cook would try his hardest and that at least would be appreciated.

When we dragged ourselves out of the jeeps at the camp the party declined the offer of our airy bathroom in favour of a basin wash-up. Then they sat on the forms at the bare wooden table in anticipation of their meal. The moment had finally come.

Footsteps sounded, approaching from the direction of the kitchen area, and by the squeaking of the new hob-nailed boots with their steel horseshoe heels I knew they belonged to one of the temporary helpers from Keswick. As he came into the room with the first plates I could hardly force myself to look at their contents but when I did, trying to appear nonchalant, I must have given a noticeable start accompanied by what I'm sure was an audible gasp.

In place of the fried sponge cake or the dehydrated potato camouflaged with tomato sauce and set alongside a small cube of bully beef, was the most sumptuous meal I'd seen that year. Sizzling roast lamb, golden baked potatoes, fresh bright-green peas, and just the right amount of saddle-brown gravy, filled the room with such a mouth-watering aroma that it forced an elated "I say—by Jove!!" from the Englishmen. I couldn't believe my eyes as more plates were carried in by the wooden-faced old soldier until everyone was served. I wondered where on earth it had all come from, and what a dark horse old Ivan was. Certainly some explanations were called for. Dessert was yet to come but a tin of peaches with unsweetened condensed milk could fix that part up if need be. We would see soon enough. In the meantime I suppressed the impulse to leap up and rush into the kitchen to see what incredible things were going on there while the the first course was devoured at a great rate by the ravenous scientists.

The empty, polished plates were duly collected, including mine which normally would have remained where it was indefinitely unless I took it up myself, and the squeaky steel-heeled boots heralded the arrival of whatever was to follow. I crossed my fingers under the wooden boards of the table and casually glanced at the first two plates. This was absolutely fantastic. They were heaped with at least a sixty-five-degree wedge of apple pie, baked on top to a honey-brown hue studded with sugar embedded in the glaze coating, with an ornamental edging on the slightly-raised crust, and a large dollop of white, creamy foam twirled to a peak and placed accurately over the apex. This time the expressionless face of the man from Keswick Barracks had the suggestion of a twinkle in his eyes as he placed the food in front of the general and Wynne. A glimmer of understanding began to dawn in my mind as his bright eyes met mine before he returned to the kitchen for more pie. After this a huge tray of iced cup-cakes, apple turnovers, chocolate fingers, and meringues arrived as a pot of coffee was placed on the table by old George Greenwood himself.

The chief scientist began to lean back, as one who is well satisfied often does, until he realised just in time that his wooden bench didn't have a back, and instead supported himself with his hands on the seat. I imagine he couldn't have stood upright then if he had tried. Turning slowly to me he observed that he was "awfully glad to know you chaps eat so well out here", to which I replied that it did help quite a lot.

Before I joined the party outside in the cool air to discuss the day's events, I just had to get some answers, so I strolled into the kitchen (at about twenty-five kilometres an hour) when their backs were turned. There, busying himself at the kitchen table, stood a very sheepish George

Greenwood, hands still white with flour and a barely-concealed grin on his face. During the early afternoon the wily George had looked for Ivan to offer to do the tea for him, but much to his relief couldn't find him anywhere, and so just took over. Asking him why he didn't ease our minds at Pimba by at least mentioning that he had some culinary ability, all I got was the old reply, "never ever volunteer for anything in the army". I couldn't ask him quickly enough if he would care to join our party permanently if we could fix it with his Keswick Barracks headquarters, and I was elated when his offhand affirmative answer told me our catering worries were over. I had no doubt whatsoever that I could keep him even if it meant getting a little help to swing it from the general himself; British army or not, he still had an influential rank.

We all discussed the beginnings of the multibillion dollar (or pounds, as it was at that time) project until far into the night. Afterwards I had a conversation with Spud Murphy, the official car driver. It appeared that pieces of the car lay strewn all the way from Port Augusta to the camp, in the form of broken springs, exhaust muffler and half the pipe, and part of the drain plug. The sump was so bent that the remaining piece of plug was seeping oil at a great rate from the damaged threads and a hairline fracture radiating away from it. The petrol tank had also received a bad dent. Altogether it was out of the question to attempt the return trip in the car.

That left only two alternatives. We would either have to take them back in our jeeps, or arrange a passage on the cattle train from the west in the morning. Spud had withheld the news up till now but when everyone was made aware of the problem, all agreed the train would be the best method for their return to civilisation and would not interrupt our work. We found out when the train would be passing through Pimba and arranged for it to be stopped, then we could at last get into our swags for what was left of the darkness. To ascertain the railway schedule, we simply drove to the siding at about two o'clock in the morning and woke the station master. I had been making regular trips there a couple of times a month to cut his and the fettlers' hair, so I knew just where his bed was.

Everyone was up bright and early, I think in anticipation of what George might have on for breakfast, and when the time came to go, the car's load was transferred to the jeeps. We saw the party off as they climbed on to the train among the cows. We would order a flat-top carriage later and drag their vehicle on to it with our truck for dispatch by rail to Adelaide.

Next came the job I had been anticipating as having top priority ever since I heard of this whole business at the Melbourne Observatory's mantelpiece: the establishment of an accurate pinpoint on the surface of the earth from which all the surveys we would be doing could originate. This could only be achieved by a long series of precise astronomical observations involving a week of careful readings on to stars at night, with the days spent in making calculations. I intended to arrive at a great number of final results, the mean of which would be the most accurate latitude and longitude for my chosen point of origin that I could possibly achieve in the field. The point was to be at the trig station named Marsella by surveyor Brooks, after the Marsella dam, one of the early attempts by the first station owners to collect water. This trig station was near the south-eastern extremity of our work and from it we could build up a well-proportioned network to extend north-west over our entire area. Not only did everything have to start from a point in latitude and longitude but also from a direction or bearing aspect, and as I could see from Marsella to Pearson's Hill, a good reference place, this also favoured my choice. Marsella was on a rise in the country ten kilometres from the Ponds back along the tracks leading to Port Augusta and a kilometre or so across the saltbush from them. I remembered that as I drove the big truck up on the first trip from Adelaide I couldn't help noticing the distance to the horizon as I slowly passed the station. When I saw it, I knew it would soon become a trig hill at least, but it was then too early to visualise it as the foundation on which the following years of work would be built.

For a week after the lightning visitors had gone, every night saw me silhouetted against a background of brilliant stars set in an inky sky. A level skyline stretched right around me, and I had an unobstructed view as I stood at my theodolite with the telescope aimed at the heavens. The lustre of the stars was increased by the complete absence of the moon, a condition for which I had waited before starting my programme. Many more stars were thus made visible, which helped considerably in the necessary locating and identifying of each one to be observed. A compact army short-wave wireless joined by an array of leads to a huge bank of dry batteries, nestled on the rocks around the point of origin, and gave me accurate time signals. These were necessary for the stopwatch timings of the transits of the stars as they passed the fine spiderweb crosswire in the telescope, also vital to the calculations. Another wire ran from the theodolite to the battery in the jeep to illuminate the optical micrometers for reading the angles. An open field book and pencils for entering the figures lay next to the radio. A pencil had to be used, for at times even in this country, a night dew dampened the paper so pen work was out of the question.

Not a sound could be heard other than the occasional scrape of my old boots on the rocks and only the light from my torch broke the darkness which, apart from the starlight, was complete. It was a scene of absolute peace, but I was fully occupied aiming the telescope, clicking stopwatches, setting and reading micrometers, and noting it all down in my book. Occasionally I could sit down on a rock to wait a few minutes for a star to appear at a pre-calculated angle and time, and in those moments I could appreciate my good fortune in being chosen to carry out this work, and think about the dozens of events leading to this end. I knew that everything I had done in my life until now had been guided by some unseen hand which led me unerringly to this destination. Had any one of the hundreds of decisions and incidents been different, then this goal might not have been reached and another turning at a crossroad could have led who knows where.

The hours were so fully occupied that midnight slipped away quickly, and in the early morning it was time to return the delicate instrument to its box, pack up the books, watches, chronometer, and tripod and turn the jeep on to the wheeltracks for the trip back to the silent camp. On some nights different members would accompany me to book the readings; Ivan, Harold, and Frank were always eager to come.

The bearing or azimuth observation needed to establish an accurate true meridian was part of this week's work, so a referring lamp had to be set up exactly over the concrete block we had cast at Pearson's Hill when we first arrived at the rocket range. Mick Waterland and Ozzie knew what was to be done so after an early tea they headed off with their Lucas lamp to Pearson's Hill to set it up in good time. I had spent the day precalculating a complete night's programme of stars for this phase of the operation. Ivan and I drove off in the other direction to Marsella and eventually all was ready—all except the expected light from across the open country. Without the light the whole night's star programme would be useless. Maybe they had trouble on the way out and would be there soon. I set the telescope to the altitude arrived at in my calculations and sure enough, there was the star waiting in the field of view, but still no lamp shone over to us. To show them which way to aim their beam in case they weren't sure which rise Marsella was on, we flashed our lamp in their direction and scanned the part of the skyline where I knew they must be. Any moment their answering ray of light would appear and I could get on with the readings, or so we were still saying four hours later as each star came and went, taking with them pages of calculations. When the last star scheduled bid us farewell as it passed from its critical position for observation, we packed up and drove off slowly across the gibbers wondering what had gone wrong. Perhaps they had got into a hopeless bog in one of the still-wet, bottomless depressions resulting from the flood, and were covered in cold mud digging their vehicle out. We'd soon see.

Reaching the Ponds we looked about for their jeep and when we didn't find it among the rabbits bobbing around the flat we inspected their stretchers, without success. They were still out on the plains, so at two in the morning it was back into our jeep and off to Pearson's Hill to look for them without losing any more time. Within several kilometres, headlights stabbed at us from the pitch-black night and eventually we stopped alongside each other. No mud-caked figures greeted us, and the vehicle was spotless. Mick, huddled in his army overcoat, asked where we had been all night. All they had seen from Pearson's Hill for hours was the revolving beam from an airport lighthouse in about the direction of Marsella, but no sign of our Lucas light. Ivan and I couldn't help laughing as we explained that we had shone the roving beam, probing the horizon for them, and that the nearest airport was 480 kilometres away. I think I was the first to stop laughing as I thought of all those figures down the drain, which would have to be redone in time for the next evening.

The following night the light from Pearson's Hill once again failed to shine and a repeat performance brought us to the camp to search in vain for the lightkeepers. Going off once more to look for them at two in the morning at least brought us the satisfaction of finding a pair of mud heaps wearily digging away at a larger mound in the rough shape of a vehicle almost down to the mudguards in a gilghi. Ropes tied to the tow-hook of our jeep, which was still on the raised, stony surround of the small depression where Mick and Johnny were wallowing, soon eased the situation. Then we all went home for a very early morning swim in the dam, boots and all. Ozzie had politely allowed Johnny to take his place on this trip, an arrangement which brought lasting pleasure to him, and was the source of many a joke to come. Even if we were getting nowhere at this rate, it was at least keeping me in wonderful practice with the sums.

One week and dozens of observations later saw the final

result: a value in figures for the latitude and longitude of the Marsella origin, converted to metric equivalent, and the most precise bearing between it and Pearson's Hill I could obtain. All the time the obvious magnitude and importance of this whole concern, strengthened by the atmosphere left behind by the whirlwind visit of the general, spurred me on to spare nothing in my efforts. I was confident that the figures I had before me on our "office" table in the Ponds homestead would stand up to any searching test of time.

Everything we would be doing for years to come would now be directly connected with this starting point, and the building of the framework to cover the whole area for hundreds of kilometres could really get under way in earnest. This framework would control the complete overall layout of a rocket range in Australia.

7
First Human Contacts

On returning to camp one afternoon we were astounded to see we had a visitor, a motorcyclist on his way to the opal fields at Coober Pedy, 300 kilometres to the north-west. Arriving at our camp gave him an equal shock for when he left Port Augusta he didn't expect to see anyone until he got to the fields. Even then, only a relatively few opal gougers would have been there at that time, living in holes in the ground.

We asked him where his belongings were and he indicated a small canvas haversack roped to a carrier alongside a gallon tin of petrol. Admittedly it was hot weather with not much need for blankets, but this looked altogether a little too frugal to include essential food and water. He showed us the contents: one army water bottle, a pint tin of oil, and a brown paper bag of dates. Apart from the can of fuel that appeared to be all his luggage. We always thought we travelled light but we vowed to cut down in future so as not to be outdone by this man. Asked about tools or patching gear for his tyres, he produced from his shirt a rag bundle holding a screwdriver, shifting spanner, and patches, with a small geological pick protruding from both ends of the kit.

We installed him at our table for a meal which he devoured as if he hadn't eaten for a week, and we hoped George's cooking wouldn't spoil him for his bag of dates on the rest of the trip. He camped with us on the stone verandah of the old homestead for the night and went out to his motorbike at first light. There on its side on the ground was his cycle lying in a pool of red dust soaked with petrol which had leaked out of the tank after it had fallen off its stand. We wondered why it had fallen as there had been no wind and the ground was firm when he left it, but on further investigation we detected a crack along a seam of his spare petrol tin, jarred apart by the rough trip up. The petrol had trickled down the stand to soak and soften the dirt, slowly allowing the whole thing to subside and topple over.

Of course we supplied him with a stronger, slightly larger tin, filled it with petrol, and wrapped it in sugar bags to cushion the banging on his carrier. Then we filled his tank, heaped as much food as he could carry on his bike and in his shirt front, and off he chugged away to the west. We never saw him again but a year later we heard from the "fields" that a motorcyclist had dragged himself into their area. After a week of disillusionment, he had made off once again, this time for Alice Springs. We hoped he'd learned a little more about basic survival since he had been our guest; I often thought that but for the advent of our project at that particular time, the slight rise near our camp could easily have sported a second grave alongside that of John Henry Davies.

It wasn't long before another unusual thing happened, unusual for that country at least. It started to rain. Black clouds built up to turn one afternoon almost into night when Johnny and I were nearly fifty kilometres from camp over the rolling tableland. We had been reading some angles with the theodolite at another trig rise. When a few huge spots of rain fell on the open jeep we decided to attempt to reach the camp before things started to happen

63

as they were obviously going to from the ominous look of the sky. We weren't concerned about getting wet but after rain in this country the bottom would surely fall out of the ground and a return trip would be impossible in a vehicle. We still had a long way to go when the downpour came in earnest. The jeep left a snakelike track in the softening red mud as we weaved around the dozens of small depressions already filling with water. The gibbers covering the intervening ground were a small help and with the momentum of the little vehicle we just managed to keep going as the wheels spun in the softer parts. By the time we reached the watercourse alongside our camp, it had begun trickling and we needed an extra burst of speed to splash our way across its stony floor. We quickly carried the instruments and the important field notebook inside the old homestead and then at last we could take off our saturated shorts and boots to the sound of the deluge beating on the old iron roof.

That was the start of several days of inky skies emptying cataracts of water on our lonely little camp; almost a year's quota of rain had fallen by the time it eased. Day by day we watched the watercourse over which we had driven become a swollen raging torrent. The water poured into the channel from hundreds of square kilometres of catchment, gaining impetus until it surged past the camp in a boiling turmoil. The wild flood was thankfully still a good three metres below our little rise but on the other side of us the water from the main stream diverted into a second course, cutting off any possible exit to the west and submerging the Ponds dam completely. In a matter of several days from the time when the rain had really set in, our camp and the homestead were converted into a complete island as the waters again met further to the north. These conditions, added to the floods of the previous year, would give a new lease of life to the usually dust-dry tracts of saltbush and mulga trees struggling for existence on rare showers of rain, but I could also foresee difficulties besetting our work for many weeks to come: endless bogs, shovelling mud from the wheels of vehicles resting on their chassis in the red mess, and arduously negotiating miniature lakes and streams of water where once we could have gone in a straight line.

During the period we were marooned on our "desert island" I was able to catch up with many calculations and start the first map to be drawn for this whole venture. I carefully titled it "Proposed Development Area" and had it well under way before I could attempt the fieldwork again. Outside on the flat a number of reinforced concrete cones, forty-five centimetres long, were setting in moulds with brass Survey Corps plaques cast in the narrow ends. The cones were to be used for permanent survey marks for later reference when it came to laying out sites for the actual building.

As Easter drew near the creek stopped flowing, but the deeper holes were still full and the larger lakes brimmed over with water, fresh at the top, becoming saline towards the bottom. One large lake, named Richardson, was up to fourteen metres deep in parts when we carried out a series of soundings with a long wire attached to a heavy brass plumb-bob. Each depth we sounded was fixed in position by two parties on the bank who, when given a signal, took bearings on the small boat we borrowed. Joe Stanford, who had occupied the Ponds out-station ten years before, later told me that he used to ride a horse across that same lake, a feat which at the time I couldn't bring myself to believe.

At the beginning of the Easter week I decided to try to get on with some more work in the field; an area sixteen kilometres west was showing up on the plans as the next place to concentrate on. Frank and I headed off from the homestead in that direction to try to reach the locality over the boggy intervening country. All we carried on the jeep was a theodolite and tripod, survey bag and pegs, and the usual packet of dry slimming biscuits for emergencies.

The first main hazard was a large cane grass depression known as Fred's Camp Swamp, about a kilometre in diameter and still full of water. It lay nearly one-and-a-half kilometres from the Ponds over a small escarpment. After scrambling the jeep up the stony parts of this ridge, we dropped down on to the edge of the huge circular sheet of water. I never found out just who Fred was, but assumed he must have been a boundary rider for the main station at some time in the past. I had to admit he had camped on a nice-looking area. Swans floated about between the spikes of cane grass protruding out of the water, and the ground covered with saltbush and gibbers sloped up to higher tableland country all around. At the time I couldn't possibly have foreseen that the higher tongue of land separating the Ponds from Fred's Swamp was to become one of the most important sections of this vast and costly scheme.

Keeping to the stonier parts we edged around the perimeter of the basin to its far side and drove up the rocky western slope. On its summit was a quartzite cairn erected by Brooks over one of his early trig stations. It was named Hiern Hill; after erecting a beacon there we would be returning to it many times to read angles to other points as our network expanded. Right now we were hoping to travel another sixteen kilometres to fix the position of an undulation we had observed from Pearson's Hill some twenty-four kilometres to the south-west.

Then came a series of some of the worst bogs we'd been in for a long time. There seemed nowhere to turn at times to evade soupy-looking patches and the vehicle's momentum was often not enough to lunge it across, so down we went, again and again. Each bog meant we had to climb out into the red mire with shovel and lifting jacks, dig a space around each wheel large enough to fill with gibbers and saltbush pulled out by the roots, and raise each wheel laboriously in turn to pack the herbage under it. With the tyres deflated to sloppy proportions, an hour or two mostly saw us out of each bog. By mid-afternoon, nearly ten hours' drive from the swamp, we reached the highest ground we'd been making for. We began the theodolite work after we removed the gluey mud from our hands by scraping them on the sharp metal of the bonnet and wiping them on an old onion sack used as padding

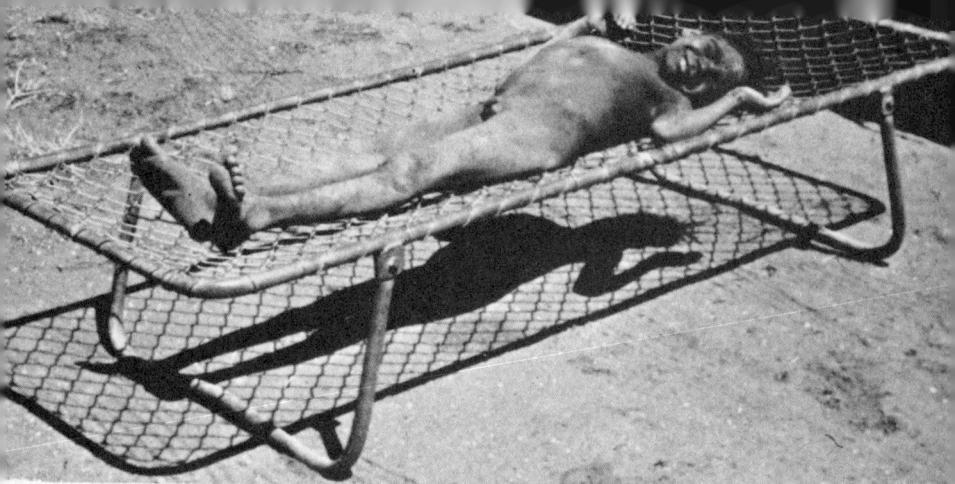

for the instrument tripod.

The effort had been well worth it as we could see our beacon silhouetted on the skyline at Pearson's Hill and also another two we'd erected on other prominent features. From the angles read, we could accurately calculate the relative position of the peg we hammered into the ground, over which we then proceeded to build a stone cairn to sight back to from the others.

Our boots were moulded over with an enormous globule of mud starting from our knees, and the jeep was one shapeless mass from the sides down. The wheels were all but hidden from view and the pedals inside had turned into great knobs of clay, making it a wonder that they still operated.

The sun was dipping on the western horizon by the time we finished and clambered aboard to tackle the return trip to camp. At the rate we came out it would be well into the early hours of the morning before we made it, if we did at all, so we took our leave of the cairn and slowly trundled off. Several large sticky patches at the lower reaches of the rise made us take a course involving a large circular sweep westerly before turning in a direction which would lead back to camp.

It proved our downfall when, after sloshing along for a kilometre or so, we chanced a shortcut across a depression instead of keeping to the western rim as we should have done. Down to the mudguards we went. Out of the jeep and into the mire again, where the new lot of mud added to our first layer and made each step a five-minute operation. Under the fresh coating the old mud was hardening like cement on our arms and pulling out by the roots hairs which had welded into the miniature bricks. Before one wheel had been attended to, the sun had gone from sight and with it went completely our hopes of sleeping at our own camp. Any thoughts of negotiating the custard-like ground were dispelled, but at least it would be nice to subside into the mud for the night with the jeep out of this mess, on stony ground, so we carried on working by torchlight. An hour before midnight saw the wheels

A downpour of rain helped me drive on to the top of sandhills for trig survey (*top*) . . . but (*bottom*) made Paradise Well a little moist on Easter Sunday

cleared enough to pack under them the pile of saltbush we gathered, and it was worth an attempt to drive out on to a patch of gibbers near by. Tentative acceleration seemed to have a slight effect on the vehicle so, becoming braver, we carried on as the floppy tyres folded over the roots. We progressed fully twenty centimetres before the angle of the jeep made the wheels slide off the scanty wooden track we had arranged by the blurred light of a mud-smeared torch. It was at least as deeply embedded as before.

One look was enough and we slumped down on the seats completely incapable of any more work for that day. We took out the packet of dry biscuits after scraping more mud off our hands on the edge of the shovel. The number of bogs all day and this last effort took their toll; the remainder of the night was going to be bleak and cold. We read about the slimming properties of the biscuits on the packet, but with nothing to eat all day we felt we weren't really in need of this particular information. The crunching of the dry wafers was the only sound to be heard in this otherwise deathly-quiet and gloomy spot.

Suddenly, as if there were no end to the surprises this country had to offer, a beady eye of light appeared in the blackness, approaching us from over the rim where the sun had set six long hours before. We sat there speechless, peering through the gloom as the tiny glow drew nearer; even our crunching stopped, as hungry as we were, and our jaws sagged open. Finally the faintest outline of a figure took shape behind the light. This just couldn't be true, but in a matter of minutes a gruff voice penetrated the night with the one word "G'day". Endeavouring to sound equally casual we nonchalantly returned the greeting as if this were an everyday occurrence in a town and not happening in quite such a unique setting.

Jack O'Brien, the old boundary rider, as he turned out to be, had been trying to get to sleep in his tin hut at the south-western extremity of the main sheep station, just out of our line of sight over the rim. Noise carries a long way on still, desert air, and the periodic bursts of engine revving from our attempts to get out of the bog had interrupted him until he finally came to see what all the commotion was about. We were waiting for him to ask us if we were bogged as so many others would have done, voicing the obvious, but old Jack took a more practical line, informing us that we were to be his guests for the rest of the night. Clutching our muddy packet of slimming wafers we followed him over the rise and soon saw his little iron shack in the beam of his torch.

It was a two-roomed structure, with a dividing wall made up of four greasy woolpacks held together with baling clips. One side contained his bag bed and blackened hurricane lamp, while the other was free for his eating and cooking arrangements. When we got inside he began to dig into the dirt floor with a stick from his firewood heap by the bushman's stove; for a while we wondered what this operation was for. Soon a leg from the corner of a sheepskin mat emerged, which he tugged until the whole floor-covering was revealed after being submerged in dust for many a long month. By way of explanation he mentioned that he had noticed our lack of blankets and thought the rug would do for one of us. More bedding could be found by digging into the floor of his bedroom, which we did while he made up his fire for a billy of tea. Actually we were pleased to see dry dust as a change from the soupy, gluey mud we'd been wallowing in all day long.

After a yarn over our tin mugs of hot tea and the wafers which we were able to share, Frank and I lay down on the dusty ground, half under the plank table, and drew the "bedclothes" over ourselves. The fleeces, although a little less dusty after the shaking we'd given them, were filled with prickles from the saltbush paddocks where their original owners had been wandering about in search of feed. It took a little manoeuvring to adjust them so that patches free of thorns could be tucked round our faces. The drying mud on our arms and legs stayed where it was or came to rest in the churned-up bulldust of the dining-room floor, but we were at least lying down indoors out of the cold night air, something which an hour before had seemed impossible.

After a breakfast of tea and some pieces of salt mutton with damper and plum jam, we all trooped back over the rim in the morning sunlight to see that our jeep hadn't moved at all throughout the night and that the mud had set like junket around the wheels. This helped with our shovelling because, as each heap of the red mass was removed, the remaining hole stayed open instead of immediately filling up with liquid mud again, as it had done the night before. The utmost effort was needed to move each shovelful because of the suction on the underside of the metal. Once when trying to pull one foot out to move to a new position, I discovered this action had left my boot in the mud. It took a quarter of an hour of shovel work to regain it from a depth of forty-five centimetres.

By far the worst part of the whole thing was fast becoming painfully apparent: with every movement of our encrusted limbs, the layer of hardened clay from the day before was constantly being disturbed. The hairs had been welded solidly into "ceramic tiles", and as each tuft was pulled out by the roots, the arms and legs somewhere deep down in their casings were feeling the strain. It was a problem I'd never encountered before or since but right then it added very considerably to our plight.

The overnight hardening had really helped and after each wheel had at last been doctored, the first try with the engine was enough to lurch the vehicle forward on to higher stony ground. We thanked old Jack for his hospitality, not knowing that in a short time we were going to play a big part in helping him in return, and headed once again for our camp.

In the sunlight we could pick the safest ground surface easily and after several close shaves we managed to reach camp by early afternoon, only to find it deserted except for George. It was wonderful to hear of their concern; everyone, complete with binoculars, had spread out in the remaining jeeps in the general direction we had taken, to search for us when we failed to return by morning. That we'd been bogged they were certain, and they knew that another vehicle would be an asset in helping to extricate us.

There was nothing we could do to advise them of our arrival under our own steam. We had not eaten anything but some waistline-preserving biscuits and salt-junk since the previous morning, so we were very grateful to George for our mid-afternoon meal. Then came hours of soaking in the dam to loosen the armour coating from every part of us which had been exposed. I'm sure we'd never had such red-raw tender skins since we were each a fortnight old.

By dusk the others had arrived back home for fear they should get into a similar predicament in the gloom; in fact they had all been in and out of bogs all day, but with the difference of having a second vehicle and tow ropes to help each other. Many thanks for their efforts were given and after we related our story, they wondered if our sheepskin blankets had in fact still been occupied by the sheep.

8
Doing Unto Others

Although this particular section of the rocket range was on a sheep station, we had yet to see a sheep and I wondered just what it would have eaten had there been one. It was too early in my contact with these areas to know that far from being poor, this was excellent sheep country where lambs kept coming in wonderful condition. This station carried over a hundred thousand head on its 4000 square kilometres. Eventually one-third of it would be acquired from the owners but still leaving them the grazing rights. At that time it was a Kidman property named Arcoona, and the main homestead lay only twenty-six kilometres north of our camp, although we hadn't yet had the time to either see it or meet the people. That time had now come as we thought the most sensible way of obtaining fresh meat would be to buy a sheep from them each week, instead of ordering it up on the "Tea and Sugar" train at Pimba.

This "Tea and Sugar", as it was known, was a sort of travelling grocer, fruiterer, butcher, draper, and anything else required by the families of the gangs of fettlers living along the railway line from Port Augusta to Tarcoola. Any sheep or cattle stations on the way were also supplied and mailbags, saddles, sewing machines, windmills, or safety pins would be loaded on to the long train after being ordered by various means such as Flying Doctor radio signals, letters, or party telephone lines joined to the main link along the railway. People from some homesteads would have to travel hundreds of kilometres to meet the train for their deliveries. Trucks dragging big trailers for items such as stock tanks, troughs, and building supplies would be waiting at their particular sidings for loading direct from the "flat top" goods carriages, and horses and pack animals would arrive to collect smaller things for Aboriginal outcamps. Even a camel wagon would occasionally turn up to carry supplies to some dam-sinker's remote tent. Most ordinary foodstuffs could be bought direct from their appropriate box-cars, except in cases such as ours when extra orders would have to be made in advance to cope with large quantities. One of our jeeps would often be waiting at the Pimba siding to collect our orders which we would telegraph down to the Port using the railway system.

It was a most useful feature of the Commonwealth Railways in this country but getting our meat from over a hundred kilometres away when we were living in the middle of a sheep station seemed like bringing "coals to Newcastle". So we decided to pay a visit to the Arcoona homestead, which was managed by Mr Michael Mudie and his wife, who, although they knew of our activities, had in turn been too occupied with their own work to make the first move. The rain and the boggy track between us had not encouraged either party to visit the other, but one fine morning Johnny and I were on our way. After getting bogged several times and having many near misses, we topped a rise from which we could see the station's headquarters spread out before us. A huge fresh rainwater lake spread out to distant banks on the far side of the cluster of buildings and the high-water level was barely a metre below the rock barricade fence downhill from the house. This was Lake Arcoona according to the scant information on the aeronautical map covering this area; we had already passed Lake Richardson where our surveys had brought us, and Swan Lake covered with black swans, and this was the next and last in the chain.

Our first impression was one of amazement, for instead of seeing a tin hut as we had at old Jack's camp, or a small stone building like the one we lived in at the Ponds, a miniature village sprang into view. There were houses, outbuildings, horse stables, and a huge woolshed complete with adjoining loading ramps, hoists for wool bales, a maze of holding yards and races leading into the shearing cubicles, and vehicles standing everywhere. Even an old grader with great iron wheels and rings for controlling the blade height stood near a killing gambrel hanging from a long log lever, with the rusting trace-chains lying in the dirt, free from the last old draught-horse which had once dragged it along.

Down the slope we propelled our spattered little vehicle, leaving a trail of soggy clumps of mud as they fell away from the wheels, and pulled up without the use of brakes outside what appeared to be the main establishment. Michael Mudie was already waiting for us as we lumbered our heavy, sticky boots out of the open-topped jeep. He was an exceptionally pleasant, quietly-spoken man, tall with slim build, and I knew instantly that we would all get on well together, as is almost always the case when bushmen meet. After a few handshakes we were guided to his door, and his wife had already laid out a table with tea and scones. I couldn't wait to ask him where all the sheep were, and was informed they were in another paddock. We'd travelled many kilometres and hadn't arrived at the end of our "paddock" so we gathered his enclosures each covered hundreds of square kilometres. We hadn't sighted a boundary at this stage but he assured us the station was fenced to keep the sheep in, or the kangaroos out, which-ever way you looked at it. Ever since, on being asked by newcomers to Woomera where all the sheep were, we could always reply that they were in another paddock.

We related the circumstances of our meeting with old

Jack, which he already knew about from a message relayed along the top wire of one of these elusive fences used as a party telephone line. A little telephone pack was clipped to the wire, and when its handle was cranked it operated the bell on the other end. This whole system broke down when the rain shorted out each post, and in season, occasional tingles were heard as lightning hit the fence. Then we began the complicated negotiations about the weekly sheep rations. We would indicate over the wire when we would like one and call in on our way past, fitting in the surveys in that direction with our meal requirements. This arrangement would also be useful for them as we would pick up their mailbag or goods from the "Tea and Sugar" when we were due to visit. At the same time it would be obvious that we were buying our meat locally, and not openly rustling sheep.

After being filled in with some earlier history surrounding the Ponds homestead and the coaches plying between the Port and Kingoonya, we made our way back to camp in daylight hours. It was still a touch-and-go operation trying to drive anywhere in a motor vehicle so soon after rain.

The arrival of Easter weekend means a cessation of usual work for most people but when it came that April we were so occupied with urgent work that we were scarcely aware it was upon us. In the morning of what I discovered later was Easter Sunday, I turned the nose of the jeep in a northerly direction to locate a site for another trig beacon in an area indicated by the plans I had been drawing as the work progressed. Nine kilometres out, adjacent to Pearson's Hill, I came to a windmill which Michael Mudie had called Paradise Well. It was sited in a low-lying depression for the shallower digging of the well, so the ground was extra soft. The rainwater had collected around it and although the days of sunshine had given a false impression of a hard surface, the underlying mud was virtually bottomless. I had at least been able to point out to the boys the track which I'd be taking, thinking of the still-

75

vivid memories of the night at Jack's, so I wasn't too concerned at venturing closer to inspect the level of water in the well.

It was well filled and the pump had the near-by stock tank abrim with clear water. Back in the jeep I drove a very short distance, not horizontally but quite vertically down into the soup once more, and wondering when I was ever going to get the hang of this country I plunged into it again with the all-but-worn-out shovel. This was nine o'clock in the morning and I was still digging and piling rocks in the mire at six that evening when the faithful old three-ton truck, which had first brought me into this place, lumbered into view accompanied by another jeep. The big winch drum and steel cable on the front was all I really saw from my vantage point halfway under the wheel I'd been working on for three hours. In a matter of minutes the cable was attached and the strain taken. I was glad to see Max was at the controls and not Ozzie, knowing it would be just his luck to pull my jeep in half as the mud built up like a soft brick wall which followed the little car out on to dry ground.

Later, in answer to a signal from Keswick Barracks, I replied by telegraph that I had indeed spent Easter Day in Paradise.

Then more visitors came to our camp in the form of the Director of Works in South Australia, Mr Haslam, and several engineers who would be involved later on with the construction programme. I took them on a tour of the scenic beauty spots including the mud hole which Fred's Swamp had become, the grave of John Henry, the upper reaches of Lake Richardson, and our murky bathroom at the Ponds' dam. I showed them the area contained on my Proposed Development Area map and then, as I had already been requested by the Pimba telegraph office to supply locations for the establishment of an airfield, I drove them up on to the western escarpment to reveal for the first time the site I'd selected. Night after night the map had been taking shape as, with the help of a kerosene lamp, I often worked into the early hours of the morning.

A stretch of ground well over one-and-a-half kilometres long showed itself to be a natural choice for a landing field. The contours drawn on the map originated from my first concrete cone block, for one of the traverses pointed to the fact that it would be an ideal start for the centre-line of the runway, a fact I explained when we gathered around the brass plaque.

As it eventually came to pass, the present main north—south strip of tarmac for the airport at Woomera, which has been in constant use for the succeeding twenty-six years, revolves exactly about this number one traverse station. I did have two other suggestions in mind but geographically this was the most suitable site and I purposely omitted to mention them. One was on the Pearson's Hill tableland and the other lay nine kilometres to the east of the Ponds in the direction of my astronomical station at Marsella. Both would have added ten kilometres to a proposed rail link from Pimba which I gathered was included in the future plans. As we stood there on the open plains I was able to convince the party who would be passing the information on to other powers in Adelaide, that it was the right location.

It wasn't long after they had gone that we received word to peg out a centre-line for the airfield construction project squadron who were being prepared down south for this job. Back to the traverse-station plaque with a potato sack full of wooden pegs, I set up the theodolite, and laying off a northerly bearing by an angle from station number two, sighted through the telescope and lined in a survey waddy behind the spiderweb crosswire. The individual pegs would come later, put in with a measuring chain, but the main line was the first concern to prove the feasibility of the location. The ground I was driving over was still soft so running the line was a slower operation than usual, but eventually the line of stakes, painted white and red, was installed and it was followed by the chainage pegs.

Often when working in a westerly direction, we could travel most of the way without the slightest fear of bogging down because, much to the sorrow of the Commonwealth Railways had they known, we would clamber our vehicle up out of the mud flats on to the railroad and drive along over the sleepers. The gauge was such that one pair of wheels had to ride between the rails with the other set outside, leaving one steel track under the jeep. It was rough, slow going but at least the snail's pace could be kept up indefinitely until our working area was reached, and more often than not, after attempting to leave the line we'd become bogged within a metre or so. Of course an alert eye kept probing ahead and behind all the time for fear an occasional express train might be bearing down on us, but as the tracks could mostly be seen dwindling to a pinpoint either way, we felt safe from this hazard.

One time proved exciting when, after mounting the inner wheel over the rail to drive off, both front wheels became embedded in the mud leaving the rear ones still on the track. We had never worked so fast to free the wheels from a bog. Every movement of the jack was interrupted by an anxious glance along the line. Old discarded sleepers helped considerably in this particular operation in place of the usual greasy gibbers and saltbush roots.

There was a huge sandhill on the eastern side of Lake Richardson where I wanted to erect a temporary sighting beacon, as it was visible from almost anywhere for many kilometres and so a valuable help to our work. To reach its base you had to laboriously skirt around the rocky shores of the lake, being careful to stay high enough on the dry spots, and cross several small sand ridges. Frank and I had tried just before the rain had set in but could get little closer than two kilometres from it, and time didn't allow us to hike across, for it would have taken most of the day to skirt the rocks around the lake. Now the rains had gone I decided to make another attempt alone, as this point was becoming increasingly important. After clearing the lake I found I was easily able to drive over the smaller sand ridges, whereas before the tyres would churn their way down and not move forward at all, even when they were deflated. I found also that as I drew closer to the sandhill, the jeep, far from faltering, continued to travel forward and up the sandy slope to land right on the summit. Compared to the previous attempt and to later crossings of sand-dunes immediately after rain, this was incredible; no resistance was offered, and in fact wet sand became a pleasure to drive on. The small shrub I'd chopped in the scrubby creek inlet into the lake was soon planted as solidly as possible in the wet, sandy crest and I photographed it alongside the jeep to prove the feat to Frank. It would last there long enough to be an effective sighter until other points could be fixed from it, before the sand dried and was eroded away.

As if visitors would never stop descending on us — we'd had four lots so far this year — a car pulled into the Ponds one night as I crouched over my map working to the tune of old George's snores. He was the only one who actually slept in the house as he was always first up to make the breakfast fire, while the rest of us used our three tents erected outside. I laid my pencil on the protractor, slipped my bare feet into the open pair of hobnailed boots by the "desk", and clomped outside to interview these latest arrivals. Several men stiffly got out, followed more slowly by a lady whom I found later was almost ninety years of age. I ushered them inside and transferred the kerosene lamp to the dining-room table, by which time George was already out of his blankets and the crackling of sticks told us a billy of tea was on the way.

They were bound for the Andamooka opal fields which lay over 110 kilometres north of us in the country to the north-west of Lake Torrens, a stretch of dried salt extending 160 kilometres north—south. The old lady proved by far the most interesting guest we'd had so far at our establishment and this was by no means the first time she had been in this house. She told us of things that had taken place when she was a little girl ten years old, living right here in the old coaching days eighty years before. She said the house was just the same solid rock structure with its thick walls and underground rainwater storage as it had been then, with the exception of the railway-sleeper shed built by old Joe.

By this time we had put up a spare tent especially for the use of the travelling public, so after their thanks to George and the explanation that they hadn't seen enough wood for a fire of their own since nightfall, I showed them to their room.

Next morning began the futile effort to get their car started, and an inspection underneath revealed a wet patch below a small, jagged hole in their petrol tank. If this kept up the dust around the Ponds would become saturated in petrol, for everyone who passed seemed to pour out their fuel on the ground. Out came the tank and an old-fashioned copper penny and I set to work with a soldering-iron and emery paper. If a penny is heated in a fire until it is cherry-red and plunged into water, it becomes soft and can be beaten out with a hammer until quite large, working in the opposite way to steel. By midday we had the flattened coin soldered in place and the tank re-installed and refilled from our drums. Of course it was too late to make a move before dinner and well in anticipation of this, George had the meals ready. We sent them happily on their way to the fields, but not before they showed us a sample of opal from their bag because we admitted we didn't even know what opal was, apart from vaguely knowing it was a precious gemstone.

It seemed as if the stream of callers would never end; a few nights later I again laid the pencil and protractor aside as I heard a rapping on the old door. Wondering who on earth this could be as I hadn't heard the slightest sound of an approaching vehicle, I opened up to find the smiling but tired face of Michael Mudie just visible in the gloomy light from the lamp on the desk. His first words were to say that if it weren't too much trouble, he could do with a little help just then. It was almost midnight and it was beginning to appear that no one ever slept after dark in this country, but we were soon sitting on the form to the sound of crackling sticks in the kitchen. I wondered if George rued the day he ever met up with our camp, but we knew he was elated to have another mouth to feed.

Michael's story unfolded after he casually mentioned

he'd been walking over the rolling tablelands to our camp ever since dusk, as his truck had refused to start again after a long series of coughs and splutters. It was about twenty kilometres away and he had gone across country to collect our old friend Jack from his hut to drive him to the Pimba railway siding. Jack was at last pulling out of this country after many faithful years, and the west-bound train was due through at about two o'clock in the morning. By now the sun had largely dried out the drenched country and it was possible to move about more freely without the ever-present spectre of bogs of a few weeks before.

An expert mechanic in the bush, Michael had an important decision to make when his engine stopped for the last time with still about thirty kilometres to go to meet the train. Would he risk working on the engine, pulling it to pieces with no real certainty of success; or would he be sure of it and walk to the Ponds while there was still time for our assistance? Leaving old Jack huddled in the stranded truck, he had straight away decided on the sure way, and walked. Knowing this country like the back of his hand, he set out in a straight line for us and arrived at midnight.

Before our tin mugs were cold, Michael and I were heading off to the west through the black night in my jeep either to have a go at his engine, or whisk Jack to the train if time ran out. This sort of thinking is part of the bushman's way of life. With an hour and a half to spare, the black shape of the idle lorry was picked out in our headlights. Once again old Jack greeted us with a "G'day" as though we were never to meet up with him other than in the dead of night on the open gibber plains.

We set to work on the engine and when we dismantled the fuel pump a break showed in the diaphragm. We replaced it with a spare and had the engine going within ten minutes. Not once did Michael indicate any regret at having made the long hike in the dark virtually for nothing, but said he would most certainly have done the same again, in a similar position. I knew that was true; I wouldn't have hesitated either. You've got to be sure and not sorry in the bush.

With Michael and Jack in the lead I followed them into Pimba to make old Jack's train ride to Perth a certainty and was able to join in finally farewelling him from the country he lived in and loved for so long. My last words were to thank him again for his sheepskin-blanket hospitality on our fateful night not so very long before.

Top: The beacon we erected over surveyor Brooks' old 1875 Coorlay trig station. I used this in my first triangulation survey of the rocket range. *Bottom:* I often made observations to the sun to calculate bearings for the survey

9

The Project
is Christened

During this time the wheels of the army had been
turning and now, in May, they pointed to Lindsay Lockwood. He was to be posted to direct a school of army
survey in another State and would be replaced by Wally
Relf, a Survey Corps major who had been installed, the last
I saw of him, in the observatory buildings in Melbourne,
where I had first talked with the Colonel Director about
going to start some sort of a rocket range. At that time
there was no thought of Wally joining us, but now with
Lindsay going, someone was needed to coordinate the
proceedings so that we could concentrate full time on the
actual fieldwork.

Lindsay and Wally drove up to our camp together for
the former's last trip then, amid more farewells, they left
for Adelaide where Wally would generally be stationed,
allowing easier liaison with the Englishmen. As they disappeared over the hill in the direction of Port Augusta I
didn't realise it would be fifteen years before I again set
eyes on Lindsay Lockwood. I was driving from Adelaide to
Melbourne at the time in pouring rain when I happened to

Top: The first concrete block on the centre-line of Woomera's main airport runway
was set in the ground alongside Michael's famous signpost. *Bottom:* The first take-off
from Woomera. The Dakota making this historic flight churns up the dust on the new,
unsealed runway

notice a theodolite covered with a waterproof bag set up under a tree, and a pair of figures huddled under a canvas camp-sheet next to it. I stopped at the sight of the instrument and called out to ask if there was anything I could do, as there was no other vehicle in sight, when who should stand up and hurry over but Lindsay. He was soaked as he climbed into my car and explained that his own vehicle wouldn't be returning for him for several more hours. What a yarn we had sitting there out of the rain, catching up on the previous fifteen years' news. He was out of the army by then but I was still completely occupied with the project we had started together so many years before on Pearson's Hill.

That was the last time I saw him alive, because ten years later, just a quarter of a century after farewelling him on that morning at the Ponds, he died of a shocking illness in Sydney.

So it was Wally's turn to gather instructions from General Evetts and his team to pass on to me for carrying out on the site, and he would be making occasional trips up when it became necessary.

These comings and goings couldn't be allowed to interfere with our work, and no sooner had their dust subsided than I was off with the instruments across the saltbush flats to continue the vast survey programme which had so far merely scratched the surface.

Two nights later, after Lindsay's departure, I felt I just could not work on that plan another night without a spell, so I reported to my swag of blankets in the tent at a reasonably early hour and in minutes was sound asleep. Then what seemed like an instant later, but actually was just before midnight, I felt myself being shaken and an urgent voice penetrated the fog of sleep, pleading with me to wake up. There never seemed to be a dull moment here, night or day, I thought, as I sat up on my canvas sheet.

It was Ozzie, Max, and old George complete with torches, and at a glance I knew something serious was wrong. George stood to the rear holding his forearm while Ozzie made the explanations.

They had all decided to take George out for a night's spell from the kitchen to shoot rabbits, and during the process their headlights had picked up the white-reflecting eyes of a fox, which they promptly proceeded to chase. On the side mudguards of the jeeps, we'd had the workshops at Keswick Barracks install a pair of threaded bolts to take a bracket clamp for carrying emergency water and petrol cans. These were adjacent to the back seat where George had been sitting, rifle in hands, ready for a shot if and when the fox condescended to stop. A rough jolting ride it had turned out to be.

Travelling at speed over one large bump on the paddock gave their jeep a violent lurch, sending George into the air still clutching the rifle. It was quite painless until he returned heavily to his seat a split second later. Even that part had been all right but not so with the underside of his forearm which had become impaled to the depth of nearly three centimetres on one of the vertical, threaded bolts. It was not only a deep hole but it trailed off into a jagged gash as his arm freed itself, and now here he stood in my tent with the blood oozing down over his hand on to the ground alongside my swag.

If you have ever had the experience of waking from a deep sleep to be immediately confronted by such a gory spectacle, I'm sure you would never forget it, as I haven't from that day to this. From George's tone I gathered he was more than concerned about it, as were we all, so after quickly washing it with warm water and bandaging it, I readily agreed to them heading off then and there to Port Augusta for a doctor's help. It was less than two hundred kilometres away and they should make it before daylight, so the jeep was refuelled and off they went. At least we had done our best under the circumstances and I only hoped George could be with us again as soon as possible. I lay down again after their red tail-light became obliterated in the dust cloud behind them as they raced off, and had quite a job to return to sleep. The last thing I remembered thinking about was: "back to the elastic porridge".

Actually, a few stitches and a week of proper care from

85

Dr John Thompson, Port Augusta's only doctor at the time, were all that George needed before he could return to us, much to our delight, as we were running low on the scrambled eggs and Yorkshire pudding mixture. The next time Wally came up through the Port he collected George and delivered him safe and sound to his kitchen. I hitched our telephone-box pack to Michael's party wire to Pimba and asked him if a sheep could be ready to collect, as we were soon to be reunited with our cook, and I was told I could have it the next morning.

When I pulled up by the homestead I asked how Michael's truck had performed on his return after Jack's eventful night, and learned from his wife he hadn't arrived home until dawn. It wasn't because of any more engine trouble, but on his way back after leaving us at three in the morning, Michael had decided to deviate over the plains to a broken-down fence which had lost its usefulness. Threaded through the old mulga posts were nine kilometres of good wire which he could use in his horse paddock and he just thought he would pull it out with the truck and carry the rolled-up wire home with him. The fact that it was rather an unusual hour for such an operation didn't enter his mind; as he happened to be within twenty kilometres of the fence it would save wasting the trip.

While we were talking alongside the jeep, I felt a tugging at my hair from behind and turned to be confronted by a pet kangaroo which had hopped up on to the bonnet. The first thing that seemed to fascinate him was my short hair which, although a different colour from grass, could stand a nibble or two for a taste.

After tea and the scones we referred to as survey cakes, I drove off with the killed and dressed sheep wrapped up in a canvas sheet to keep the flies at bay until we could install the pieces in our own kerosene refrigerator box. At this stage we used to collect the meat ready to break up and use straight away but later on we graduated to choosing our own from a flock in a sheep yard, and taking it home alive to combat the blowflies. I was taught to first discover the condition of the animal by feeling the stub of its cut-off tail and if this was soft and full, then the meat should be better than if it came off a sheep with a hard bony stub. The number of teeth and their respective lengths had a lot to do with meat quality and in no time we were selecting fatty-tailed, "two tooth — rising four" wethers like veterans. It required a separate course to learn the correct way of killing and bleeding, skinning and butchering, and this became a weekly task which always seemed to fall to me.

The Department of the Army couldn't seem to leave us alone; although we were out of sight, we were certainly not out of mind, and Ivan was the next to go. His discharge from the army had fallen due and he made his exit from this country on Wally's return trip. As he climbed on to the jeep we were all sorry to see him go; the last word we heard him say as he pulled out, muttered in an undertone with bowed head, was "remorse".

With so many months of constant work behind us we decided to go for a picnic, and we thought we'd drive to the Andamooka opal fields, a return trip of 240 kilometres, as we'd already entertained several travellers bound for them. They had said that if ever we made the trip we must look them up, or rather down, for in those days people there lived underground in holes. Max, John, and I headed off north to call into Arcoona first where Michael showed us how to get there by a map he scratched in the mud with a stick. Andamooka certainly was a unique place with a very sparse population, none of whom could be seen above ground. Caves had been chiselled out of the slopes to form rooms and after peering into the blackness, a contrast with the glare of the sun, in quite a few we eventually located some of our friends. John eagerly opened the conversation with "Here we are; where do we dig?"

Dick Clarke had been riding on the train to Perth and happened to get talking with the mail contractor at Pimba. Interrupting his train journey he accompanied the truck to the fields and never left. He is still there thirty years later, and a sure port of call on our hundreds of subsequent visits. Doug Adams and his mother had also passed through the Ponds and were temporarily installed in a dugout but had plans to build the first house above ground in the area. This he gradually did, with pine logs and mud packing, complete with a verandah which accommodated all the passengers I brought there for many years.

Right now we had to see down an opal hole and were soon lowered on a windlass rope twelve metres into the earth through a hole about a metre square. Being used to wide open spaces I found it a most disturbing experience, and once on the bottom I chanced to look up to see a tiny rectangle of sky. I was particularly distressed when the next one was on his way down, cutting off any hope of my escape; and a feeling almost of panic proportions swept over me. This phobia was obviously what had driven me away from cities and enclosures to live and work in country in which "you could see a bull-ant for ten miles". When the others were down our interest overrode everything else, and we were soon gouging away at the walls by the beam of a carbide lamp, but of course with no results.

These fields were reputed to have been discovered by accident after a bout of horseplay at a sheep musterers' dinner camp. One station hand had tossed a quartzite gibber at a battered quartpot billy of tea owned by old Sam Brooks from Andamooka Station. His immediate reaction was to throw the stone back, but as it scored a direct hit some tea had splashed over it, washing away the dust. It revealed a glassy coating which reflected the most wonderful colours from the sun that was beating down on it. Noticing the pretty reds, greens, and yellows glistening in his hand, old Sam had decided against retaliating and put it in his saddlebag to show to people back at the main station forty kilometres away.

This stone was identified as an opal floater or gibber which had once been submerged with its opal coating, but over countless thousands of years had become exposed to the open. Subsequent weathering had allowed it to be washed down the slope, and so by searching uphill, the strata in which it had been embedded for millions of years could be discovered. It caused great excitement at the station and a return trip had taken place immediately, successful enough to locate not only other such floaters but their original home as well.

The story went that this secret was kept for over a year, and the station hands virtually became partners in the diggings which were carried out as part of the station work. Then one day, while on a spell in Port Augusta, one of the members in the plot, under the loosening effect of what he'd been sipping, had opened his mouth too wide and the cat was out of the bag.

Within weeks, dozens of prospectors had converged on the area, borne by anything from old trucks to camels, and the opal fever grew as more and more sites were uncovered. This was early in the 1930s as far as I could gather. Although the sheer remoteness of the place in those days had prevented a boom rush, the hunt was really on and growing.

Much to our delight, we soon discovered that old Sam Brooks of the quartpot billy days was still camping in a semi-dugout on a near-by rise, so it wasn't long after we surfaced from that narrow, deep hole, that we all set off to interview him in person. A typical weather-beaten old bushman with the brightest twinkling blue eyes I'd seen came out to meet us. His quiet but jolly wife and family followed him and in return for the foregoing history straight from the horse's mouth, we filled them in on our activities, of which they were already vaguely aware.

The sun was nudging the western skyline by now, telling us it was past the time when we should begin the long return journey to our camp. As we drove away we knew we'd be back again and again but we couldn't visualise then that this extraordinary little place would mushroom into a thriving settlement including motels, garages, and the inevitable places for entertainment. We also didn't know that one of old Sam Brooks' wonderful little daughters would be cruelly murdered, or that a prize opal of record proportions and lustre would be dug from one of these holes and presented in a world-publicised ceremony to Queen Elizabeth II.

Our "picnic" over, with a renewed effort we pressed on with the work once more. Midday dinner on the plains had become a ritual of stopping near a patch of ground covered more with saltbush and bluebush than gibbers, pulling out handfuls by the roots, and making a fire. An old bent billy with water out of the can went on next, hanging from a tripod which I'd made from heavy-gauge fencing wire, while pieces of George's bread were toasted. The tripod ensured the billy would never fall over and put out our tiny fire which was able to burn freely under it. After the toast was placed on a flat stone, a slab of cheese was anchored on top by a smearing of plum jam. Unconventional though it was, the whole effect was relished by us all, and a tin mug of weak tea and sugar finished it off. We had to use plum jam as this was the best "carrying" jam, for when the open tin was upended as we drove over the rough surface, it would remain unspilt. Apricot jam, on the other hand, would coat the inside of the tuckerbox with a liberal thickness of the sweet gluey mass, leaving its tin quite empty. As a change from toast, about every month we heated an open tin of stew, stirring it periodically with a twig of saltbush. This replaced the cheese and jam as a good cold weather substitute. The countryside was soon scattered with little mounds of buried, burnt-out tins alongside small piles of white saltbush ash.

One day Harold, Ozzie, and Mick went out in two jeeps to carry on with the programme of levelling. At the end of the day the three of them returned in only one vehicle. Mick reported that his vehicle had stopped for good, refusing to go at all after they had done everything possible to the dead engine. It was fifty kilometres away standing alone on the tableland with no fear of parking violations, so he and I set off with tow rope and the usual coil of fencing wire to get it. From fifteen kilometres away we could see it, so we drove towards it in a dead-straight line. Soon we were looking under the bonnet before starting the long tow. A high-tension lead wire from the coil to the distributor cap looked a bit the worse for wear at a sharp bend so we pulled it off. Cutting the same length off a piece of heavy wire, we bent it to fit and merely dropped each end into the open sockets. After that, one touch of the starter button was all that was needed to hear the engine burst into life. There were no brakes and all in all, the thing mightn't have passed a test of roadworthiness but as there weren't any roads it was driven home as good as new. The same job done in the city would have been quite expensive.

A new and rather exciting requirement and one I was eager to carry out, eventually came over the telegraph. Taking into account the relative position of the Development Area and airfield site, I had to discover a point from which rockets could be fired: this was really what the whole project was about. Although the spot first decided on had to be amended later to cope with a smaller interim range which became necessary, the operation made me feel we were really getting down to it at last.

I drove twenty kilometres west to one of Brooks' old trig rises, named Ashton Hill. By inspection of our own maps which had been taking shape, I went 6.5 kilometres due north to a particularly expansive flat area and proceeded to build a rock cairn there, fixing its position on the surface by angles to our other trig stations. Then I telegraphed a signal that it was ready for perusal by the British rocket scientists who were gradually arriving in Adelaide.

This cairn, after subsequent inspection by many selected visitors, was photographed officially and I was soon to see a reproduction of it in a well-known Australian periodical. The caption read to the effect that here was the very site on which the launching pads for the firing of the future missiles from this new range would be built.

For a long time I had been trying to think of an appropriate name for this project to use on plans and communications, instead of vaguely referring to a rocket range site in Australia, but I'd constantly rejected my ideas because of their clumsiness or unsuitability. It had to be short and easy to pronounce; preferably one word to save time and space in the countless reports, and at the same time synonymous with the purpose of the project. So it was that with a visit by General Evetts and Major Wynne-Williams a name came to light. Being polite English gentlemen they had acquired a glossary of Aboriginal words and their equivalent meanings, and they indicated that it would be a nice gesture to think in these terms, as the Aborigines were the first inhabitants of the country after all.

Running their fingers down the pages the word "spear launcher" stood out, stimulating their imagination. An excited exclamation followed, "By Jove! These Aborigines are launching spears and we are about to be launching rockets. I say, but wouldn't it be polite to refer to this place by the name for their apparatus for a similar function, and christen it 'Woomera' for the time being?" It was instantly agreed that the Aborigines would certainly be pleased with the choice, and so, temporarily, it began to appear on signals and maps until a permanent name could be found. Twenty-five years later it is still being called Woomera Rocket Range and it seems that this name will finally stick with it.

The fact that there were no Aborigines to be seen didn't make any difference. The name was certain to become a reality after the postal department cast a metal stamp using the word as a postmark, because they are expensive and they didn't want to waste this first one.

At the time the description of a woomera was asked for and we explained it as a throwing-stick which had the effect of lengthening its user's arm by about sixty centimetres, thus increasing the leverage and force with which the spear could be launched. A small barb at the rear of the stick engaged in a hole in the trailing end of the shaft, which disconnected at the instant it was ready for flight.

This title fitted in perfectly with the features we thought such a name should have, and at last Major Wynne-Williams could shorten his cables to England dealing with the progress of this enormous job of national importance. Instead of the usual "some sort of a rocket range in Australia", it appeared merely as "Woomera".

10

It's All
Too Secret

Although the country had dried out enough to enable us to drive over it without the endless plague of bogs, the lakes were still quite full, making the area seem anything but arid. About forty kilometres north of us lay a large depression filled with water; amid the herbage on its surface were swans and ducks in hundreds. We had first seen Shell Lagoon from an adjoining high sandhill called Yandandaree Ridge, the site of one of Brooks' triangulation stations. We had repositioned it for our own use because the sand had blown into a higher pile twenty metres away from his station which we found, quartzite slab, crossed circle and all, on a mound six metres lower down. At the time this would have been the highest point, so to save confusion we named our point Yandandaree New, a thing which we had to do in many other similar cases. Frank and I had first discovered the old trig at the height of a sand storm on a sunny day. We had to wait until late afternoon to read the angles from our new station to avoid the shimmer and wind which we hoped would abate. The blowing had eased before the mirage died down so we decided to have something to eat as we would be waiting there till dark, with a long drive back to the Ponds afterwards.

We mixed flour, water, and sugar together and poured the thick liquid into a frying-pan of hot fat to construct a further variation of our survey cakes. The final article was smeared with jam and eaten with a fork, but in this case the sand, still forming a swirling mist close to the surface, decided to stick to the fat. It produced a perfect substitute for double-sided sandpaper. It couldn't actually be chewed, but the chunks we swallowed gave us the roughage we'd need for months to come.

On a further visit to this hill Ozzie and I had killed a sand goanna with the shovel handle, and cooked it in the same spot for a trial taste. We had made a fire in a hole with mulga dragged up from the lower levels of scrub, and when it was full of coals, settled the goanna complete with skin and tail into them, and buried the whole thing with embers and sand. We soon found out the trouble with this arrangement when another wind storm came and went, smoothing out the huge expanse of sand comprising our kitchen floor and making it impossible to locate our "oven". After digging dozens of holes tying to find our supper, we eventually pin-pointed it and were agreeably rewarded by the taste of the white meat as we pulled it to pieces. We thought it resembled fish but declared that Yandandaree Ridge didn't seem to be the best spot to select for eating or cooking a meal.

The tracks leading to Shell Lagoon continued on to another sheep station, Purple Downs, which was a northern neighbour of Michael's Arcoona Station. Johnny and I planned on paying them a visit on the next survey to take us up that way, and one day after we'd finished establishing another trig point, we carried on to see them. The well-used station track wound between the lagoon and Yandandaree Ridge and went through a cattle grid on a fence line which was also the boundary between the two stations. We had at last seen a fence, even though only the tops of the posts were visible out of the water as it crossed

94

the northern edge of the lagoon, but of course there were still no sheep. They would have been "all in another paddock".

Eventually the track arrived at the woolshed and shearers' quarters six kilometres short of the homestead, and we continued on past them thinking there would be only a short distance left to go. The country rose slightly and as the track topped a higher undulation we saw an amazing scene spread out in front of us. There was an inland sea of water extending to right and left with the far bank just visible and the track led straight down into it. However did these people get home themselves if, of course, they could manage to leave it in the first place?

We pulled up at the water's edge on the deep, well-used wheel ruts which continued on under the surface and out of sight. The only thing to do was to try and skirt the lake to the north. After two hours of crawling the jeep over rocks and between mulga trees, we decided that the owners must have an army tank at least to move about in. The afternoon was drawing on and, as it was late June, the darkness would be on us before we got there at this rate. At last the homestead and outbuildings appeared across another stretch of water with a set of tracks leading around it to the main house.

Norman Greenfield came out to welcome us, followed by his wife, Jean, and several children, and almost without any formalities we asked them how on earth they moved about in this country. When they finished laughing at our story of how we had struggled for hours to travel the last few kilometres, they explained that their wet-weather road, mostly obliterated by sheep tracks, branched off at the woolshed, and it was a matter of minutes from there to reach home. The road we had taken led straight across the Purple Swamp, which was usually a dry, dusty flat.

This meeting was the beginning of a lifelong association with this family and their widespread relatives, many of whom owned adjoining sheep stations. The children grabbed my hand and led me up to inspect their prize pet pig named "Ermintrude", an enormous white mountain of an animal who obviously knew most of her visitors but only grunted at me. Later on, as we were eating some fresh scones in the house, I was trying to think of this huge sow's name when a mud-covered vehicle pulled up outside. I got as far as enquiring the name of . . . when their visitors appeared: a bushman and two ladies on their way to the railhead at Pimba. The ladies had been staying with the man's family on another station for a spell. I was introduced to them by name, the last one being "Auntie Ermintrude". After they were settled into the timely batch of scones and tea, someone asked me whose name I had been enquiring about, which necessitated some quick thinking. I never forgot the name of that pig again.

The children were delightful, ranging in age from a year to early teens, full of life and anticipation of things to come. Over the years I was never happier than when on my way to the station to collect those old enough to accompany me on survey trips and camps, discovering old trigs, and on occasional visits to the opal fields. On such trips we would take fresh meat and scones from the station, packed in an old tomato-sauce carton by their cook, and spend from dawn to dusk in a 150-kilometre radius searching for new sites for survey marks, erecting trig beacons, and observing angles. On one occasion we made a dinner camp-fire and cooked eighteen of the most enticing chops on a grilling wire, with a billy of tea, and a pile of scones and cakes cooked especially for the trip. With all the food placed on tin plates and everyone ready to pounce, Robby, the ten-year-old boy, suddenly remembered it was Good Friday which prevented them from eating the chops. After the long trip from the station and the morning's work unpiling a huge rock cairn, they showed what bush children are really made of by only having the scones. That left me with all the chops cooked and sizzling. They couldn't be wasted, so I had to tackle them alone. For years after, even at his daughter's wedding breakfast to which I was invited, Norman kept apologising for the lack of my "usual" eighteen-chop meal.

Finally, on our way back to the Ponds from the station,

the underside of the jeep burst into flames when we were driving as fast as the track would allow to beat the dark. The next few seconds saw us shovelling sand at the blaze with lightning speed. The steel plate protecting the exhaust pipe had become jammed full of saltbush tops and sticks in the cross-country trips, and the extra speed allowed by the station track so heated the exhaust pipe that it made all the dry foliage smoulder and catch fire. In the succeeding years this proved to be a constant problem, which was overcome by carrying a stick to poke out the collected brush at every stop. Even so, many more fires occurred, resulting on one occasion in someone on one side receiving a faceful of shovelled sand from the person opposite.

Eventually the Proposed Development Area map I had been drawing at night was finished. It was needed in Adelaide, so I had to make a trip down as it was supposed to be too secret a document to send by train. One morning we prepared a jeep by pushing out all the saltbush from around the exhaust pipe, then, dressed in my best set of rags for the trip, I left the gibber plains reluctantly, although I knew I'd be back in a matter of a few days.

Passing the "haunted grave" I camped alone just short of Port Augusta after a trip which later, when the road was improved, took only two-and-a-half hours. Then I continued on to Keswick Barracks. As I drove along the bitumen, the invisible strings attaching me to the country behind were stretched so taut that I felt I couldn't get back quickly enough. No chance of bogs here after rain, even with the low-slung city cars which would have been quite useless to us at the Ponds.

The following day I drove into Adelaide, handed the map to a head office authority who was waiting for it, and returned to my old jeep parked outside in Adelaide's main road, King William Street, where I'm sure no one had ever left a vehicle before. The multitude of signs all indicated that this really wasn't allowed but I had been so free for so long it didn't occur to me to even read them till later.

The map was to be reproduced and I would collect a

copy to take back the following day, so I spent the day helping to arrange for a transit camp to be started alongside our old Ponds homestead. This was going to be necessary in the near future, when official visitors would have to be accommodated, and it was to be run on the lines of a small tent village, headed by a young army lieutenant, Leo Riedel. Already I could see the project for which we had been paving the way all the year taking shape.

The next day I returned to the head office, having left the jeep in an area more acceptable to the parking inspectors, and climbed up the stairs to the top of the building. I discovered afterwards they had an elevator. A different man seemed to be on hand as I walked into the office and asked for the copy of the map. This well-fed person was astounded that I even knew there was such a map or project, and informed me it was much too secret to hand over. He did seem to visibly deflate when I told him I had drawn it myself as a result of my own surveys, and after several phone calls, he looked abashed as he gave it to me. These city folk have too much to worry about all the time, I thought, as I rode down in the lift which he pointed out to me, avoiding the six-storey flight of stairs. As I walked along the footpath clutching the secret map, I came to the open jeep, and still thinking of the poor man on the sixth floor, jumped in. I started to drive away in the vehicle when I suddenly discovered it wasn't mine at all. When I turned to back out I was horrified to see suitcases and things foreign to me scattered around in the back. I returned the vehicle to the kerb, grabbed the map roll, hurried out of the driver's seat before some owner screamed for the police, and set off in search of my own. Alongside was a tall van, hiding my machine two cars along. I lost no time getting out of there.

I was all set to head back to my camp and felt more free with every kilometre I put behind me. Leo Riedel would be following in due course with his convoy, now knowing better the conditions which his team would have to face and even the location of his destination, which up to then was a very vague piece of knowledge in anybody's mind,

Top: In 1947 the Adams' house (in the background of this photograph) was unique on the Andamooka opal field. It was the only one completely above ground. *Bottom:* The school at Andamooka was forced to take on older pupils in order to retain Government schoolteacher Rowland Bills

apart from the general's.

Not long after rejoining my camp, a telegraph message informed me of the intention to send up a 10,000-gallon water tank for use at the future tent "hostel", which made it certain knowledge that this place was about to grow. My two-gallon water tin on the jeep lasted me for weeks. The tank could be filled with the rainwater in the lakes through a pipeline laid across the desert and a pump installed near the "beach". When it did come, followed by many others, the water from Lake Richardson and Arcoona kept the whole project going for the next two years, which would have been impossible before the floods of the previous year. It was a stroke of pure luck that the long drought broke at the close of the second World War, when this project was born.

A site for a village was coming more and more into the scheme with every visit of the general and his party, so our attention was turned to this new requirement. I could feel the lone saltbush plains slipping away from our grasp as each new proposed development loomed up, and began feeling very much as the Aborigines must have done when Captain James Cook made his first landing near Sydney.

We narrowed the choices down to two, based on our bitter experience of what happens to sections of the country after heavy rain, but one had to be discarded almost immediately. An international regulation governing approach funnels to main airfields ruled out the one which would encroach on the necessary clear space on the extension of the chosen site for our airfield. This would be an ideal place for a construction camp instead, so our second choice became the scene of a more detailed scrutiny. It was located on a more undulating area which would give natural help for drainage purposes, and on a slightly lower level than the tableland, a feature which would be desirable for the pressure of the water later to be laid on to the settlement from storage tanks.

We still had the country to ourselves so far and one day we were visited by our neighbour, Frank Raedel, who managed The Pines outstation only fifteen kilometres

Top: Our wondrous old cook, George Greenwood, sometimes helped me to skin and dress our weekly ration sheep. *Bottom:* Our assorted pets would forget their natural differences around the condensed-milk tray

away. His sheepdog, Biddy, had just given birth to a litter of pups and he wondered if we would like one. There was food enough for one in our camp so we made our selection, naming her "Biddy's Infant", and she was to remain with us for years, shifting camp as often as we did, following the trend of our survey. In turn Biddy's Infant had her own pups distributed at various homesteads over 130 000 square kilometres of country, and with each visit she would romp about with her offspring.

One day out on the plains we discovered a half-wild cat caught up in some wire by one of the few fences, and on closer inspection found its tail had been stripped bare of skin and fur, leaving only the tapering bones. With food and care she was adopted into our camp where she lived in perfect harmony with Biddy's Infant. A kangaroo joey only a few months old came next and stayed for two years. It became quite a ritual to collect all the animals with each move. Normally natural enemies, they would all gather around a circular lid full of liquid powdered milk and sugar, and together lap up their meals. The joey met with a minor accident once, resulting in a small patch of skin being laid bare, so from one of the pelts left over from a kangaroo we had eaten, Harold cut a piece to fit and stuck it over the wound with flour and water paste. He proudly showed everyone how he had repaired our pet with "genuine kangaroo skin". The fact that it came from a red buck and ours was a blue doe was entirely incidental.

Eventually the inevitable began to happen with the arrival over the eastern escarpment of the small convoy bringing the equipment to build the transit camp alongside the Ponds. We had been on our own in the area for months and were sad to have all this descend on us but at the same time we had been gradually conditioning ourselves for just such an operation. I showed Leo Riedel where the camp could be erected to give the best services to the future temporary occupants, and in no time the army boys had a huge marquee erected with groups of smaller tents placed in perfect lines with military precision.

An airfield construction squadron headed by Flight

Lieutenant Walker was next to appear, with graders to build the dirt runway based on my former line of survey pegs. It was a relatively easy operation and the saltbush and gibbers were graded off on either side of the centre-line in a matter of days, to form a long, smooth ribbon of uncompacted dirt, 1600 metres long by forty metres wide. On completion of this, word was telegraphed to Adelaide that the Dakota standing by could now be sent with its selected party to attempt a first landing.

Days went by as replies came of the estimated time of arrival, only to be postponed, with a group of us waiting by the airstrip searching the sky with binoculars in the direction of Adelaide. One day as we waited and probed the heavens, an excited yell came from someone as he caught sight of a black speck and pointed it out to everyone with field glasses. Sure enough we all picked up the unmistakable flying object, anticipating an historic event, but this was all terminated abruptly when the wedge-tailed eagle we had been studying turned into a screaming nose-dive to pounce on an unsuspecting rabbit.

Several more E.T.A.s were telegraphed and each one saw our little group of jeeps alongside the strip at the given time. On Thursday 19 June, another scream burst from Walker, who shouted "Here she comes at last!" Everyone was quite sceptical by now and didn't even bother to train their glasses on the object, only asking what sort of eagle it was this time, wedge-tailed or a hawk. The comments only lasted a very short while, ceasing as Walker yelled that it was the first time he'd seen the sun glint off the side of a bird. Immediately all eyes were riveted on the black speck which soon grew until it could be seen without the aid of glasses.

The Dakota circled around the new airfield as a bucket of sump oil was poured on to a pile of saltbush and lit to provide smoke which would act in place of a wind-sock to indicate the direction of the ground wind. The touchdown was at the far end of the strip from us and two huge plumes of dust billowed out at the back on either side of the plane. As it came to a stop alongside our group of jeeps

101

the mountain of dry dust enveloped the entire strip before slowly settling. The landing party included General Evetts and the British scientists with whom I'd had so much recent contact, and the usual conference began. One cluster of new arrivals had been sent to inspect my site near Ashton Hill for the proposed rocket launching area, so without loss of time they were clutching on to my open jeep as I drove them fifteen kilometres across country to the rock pile.

With no time to waste we returned at a great rate along the wheeltracks to the aeroplane. Frank Cohen had been complaining of a troubled stomach for days before, and was feeling very low on that eventful day, so we arranged for him to return to Adelaide on this historic plane flight. Ozzie collected his gear from the Ponds, which was bundled aboard with him as the party climbed back in. Johnny Showers remarked that he wished he had been "crook" too, so he could also be in the first plane take-off from the Woomera aerodrome.

A strongly-accented Englishman was last to climb in as the propellers began to turn over, and just before the door was slammed shut his head and shoulders reappeared for an instant. In his ever-polite way he had remembered his manners to the last, and above the engines we all heard his perfect British voice call out "I say, thanks Walker old boy . . . jolly good show, what!"

11

A New Address

The distances we travelled out to our surveys were by
now becoming too great to retain our camp at the Ponds
and this, combined with the fact that it was becoming too
crowded, spurred Wally and I on to locate a suitable place
for another base camp. One which would be more central
to our operations as the work expanded seemed to be at an
outstation of Coondambo, 100 kilometres west and known
as East Well. Coondambo, a sizeable sheep station taking
its name from the siding on the railway line, or vice versa,
was owned by the Pick family. East Well was their woolshed, twenty-one kilometres from the main homestead. It
had a row of shearers' quarters, a kitchen, water tanks, and
everything necessary to cater for the large shearing team
who used it once a year for a few weeks. A homestead near
by was occupied by Joe Stanford and his family, the last
people living in the old Ponds homestead before we came.
  Arrangements could possibly be made with George Pick
and his sons, Hector and Ted, for us to use the woolshed
temporarily, so Wally and I drove out to initiate proceedings. We went in quite a roundabout way to make use

of the trip for some other reconnaissance work and got to within twenty-five kilometres of East Well by mid-afternoon, when the jeep stopped dead and refused to start again. We worked on the engine for three hours, checking everything over and over with no result, so Wally volunteered to start walking to the woolshed first thing in the morning, leaving me to try to make the engine go once more. We made a fire and put on a billy, ate some stew out of a tin, and rolled out our swags. I continued on by torchlight rechecking things we had gone over many times already, until at midnight I finally lay down in my camp roll after wiping the grease off my hands and arms on clumps of saltbush.

No sooner had I lain down than I was asleep, dreaming about engines, until about three o'clock in the morning when I woke and sat up. The only thing I hadn't thoroughly examined was the low-tension lead from the coil to the distributor. I had cleaned one end and replaced it under the clamping nut but I was sure I hadn't tried the other. I couldn't wait till morning, so grabbing my torch and small spanner, I took off the nut, polished the lead, replaced it on the coil, and tried the starter button. It burst into life immediately and woke Wally who was so pleased that we threw our swags into the back and headed off there and then, not daring to switch it off. We camped again, this time within sight of the buildings, for what was left of the night.

When we pulled up by his old gate Joe came out to welcome us, wondering who on earth could be coming from that direction. Soon we were inside at his table with the tea and survey cakes spread out by his wife. His nine-year-old son, Don, was glad to escape some of the school work which was carried on over the Flying Doctor transceiver, as we made the explanations. Things were arranged with the main station using the party line telephone; as the shearing was over for the year we were free to make what use we needed of the facilities. They were even looking forward to our company, and telling them we would be returning quite soon with our camp, we headed back to the Ponds along the original old horse-coach tracks.

Using a plotted position in the middle of the 130-kilometre beach on the far north-west coast of Australia between Broome and Port Hedland, and my own astronomical latitude and longitude at Woomera, I calculated a true bearing between the two. If extended around the world, it would bisect the earth, and this great circle bearing was adopted as a centre-line for the range or line of flight for the rockets. The surveys we were continuing along the general direction of this line were aimed at producing maps on a scale never before needed in this country over which the rockets would travel, so that the tracking instrumentation involved could be planned.

Shortly after our return to the Ponds we packed our few belongings on our old three-ton truck and jeeps, gathered the animals—six cats, Biddy's Infant, and the kangaroo, and relinquished our hold on the Ponds homestead. We managed to travel twenty-five kilometres before becoming bogged with the heavy truck for several hours in a muddy depression, but by late afternoon we pulled into East Well and installed ourselves as if we were just another shearing team.

The Woomera base was growing rapidly as more people came to start construction of a pipeline from the freshwater lakes to the area, pumping stations, more road access, and even an open-air gaol house. This last, resembling a large aviary, was built on the open gibber escarpment near the airfield and any occupant could see and be seen from all directions. With the inevitable arrival of crates of drinks other than rainwater, it became more of a drying-out shed.

Many immigrants, lured by the attractive wages, arrived to work there and some of them became temporary tenants of the bird cage, as their customary methods of settling differences varied from the use of knives to hoes, rakes, and shovel handles. Outside building contractors were recruited, and put in the charge of a construction manager, Frank Owen. He remained with the project on the site from that early time, finally moving into a normal

105

house after the village took shape, when his family joined him. One night Frank was sitting quietly in his tent when one of his men appeared at the opening and politely informed him that "the boys" were about to burn Henry. Frank told him that the last time he had seen Henry he didn't really look inflammable, but he would check it out. The bearer of this news item gradually sank down the tent pole to fall asleep in the dust, having cleared his conscience.

On arriving at Henry's tent and finding it empty, Frank went in search of him in the direction of a loud commotion interspersed with the occasional tinkling of broken bottles. Sure enough, there he found Henry the centre of attraction with a circle of men around him, his clothes soaked in petrol, and someone groping for a box of matches. To this day Frank is sure that Henry doesn't realise he owes his very life to the combination of the drunken reporter's split-second timing and Frank's own subsequent intervention.

Another morning, after an eventful evening of so-called relaxation from the hard day's work on the plains, a certain worker couldn't be found and a search was begun for him. This narrowed down to several temporary tin shacks, which were entered one by one. As the last was opened, a grisly spectacle was revealed: the man was hanging from the rafters by a length of wire around his throat, feet just clear of the dirt, which had been kicked to a fine powder by his last dying spasms.

It became a sort of "wild west" settlement, very different from the quiet area we had known for so many months, and we were all pleased to have moved camp away from it all. The atmosphere of open plains, hard work, and apparent freedom from city restrictions seems to foster such communities; most of the inhabitants were attracted to the place only by money, and the climatic conditions often didn't help. The frequent raging dust storms and howling wind would whip up the powdered bulldust, coating beds and blankets, personal gear and eating tables, with volumes of overburden of the consistency of cocoa. After clearing it away, it could well be back again in a matter of hours. The larger the settlement the worse the dust becomes; in our little survey camp of half a dozen, we would be lucky to tread twice on the same spot.

Incidents would be related to us on our infrequent visits back to the base for more supplies. Rations, mechanical parts, and tyres were arriving at the Ponds transit camp to cope with the swelling population, but once having left the crowded camps, we were reluctant to return. Often with a tinge of regret we realised we had started it all, but this state of affairs was really only temporary, or so we kept telling ourselves. These sorts of conditions would have prevailed during the first months of settlement anywhere, but in time things would calm down as the place became more habitable. The initial atmosphere, we were very sad to say, could never be recaptured and we were grateful for the memories that our peaceful little existence at the Ponds would bring us, and which still come clearly to mind a quarter of a century later.

Old George the cook was due back at our camp from his medical treatment any time now, we were all pleased to learn, so after each ration-sheep was killed and cut up under Joe's trained guidance, I would painstakingly render down the fat and pour it off into a sterilised army dixie to have a good supply ready for George's expert use. Out all day in the bush up to distances of eighty kilometres, fixing points by sun observations, and marking ground information on air photos of the area for later plotting on our maps, we saw little of East Well, but occasionally the fat-rendering-down sessions and field computations would give me a day at home.

Finally, just as I had the three-gallon dixie full of clean, white mutton fat, word came that George would be on the east-west train. I went off on the surveys leaving Ozzie to collect him from Coondambo, a twenty-kilometre trip each way. After dark that night I drove into the camp and greeted our expert cook by asking him how he liked all the fat. When he said that he had emptied it all out into a hole he'd dug I was quite deflated, but I still couldn't bring myself to chastise him. He told me that not knowing its

107

history, he had decided as always to start afresh with everything, and that nobody under his care would ever get food poisoning. The pot had taken me weeks to fill but all I could say was how pleased we were to have him back.

Small sub-camps were always coming into the pattern of our work and from these we radiated out again in 150-kilometre trips. No group could have led a more nomadic bedouin type of life than we did for the next two years. One such camp we made was eighty kilometres west of East Well, within sight of Kingoonya on the Trans-Australian railway line. It was from here, hidden away in the dead-finish bushes, that Harold met his future wife. Doreen Crosby was the daughter of the owner of the hotel there, and our little party of four, including Max, Johnny, and I, occasionally dropped in to have a good meal in her father's dining-room. Any work within a day's drive of Kingoonya was thereafter allotted to Harold by unanimous consent. Years later I called in to visit him and his family where they were living in Melbourne and the stories of our old camps filled the entire night, with Doreen tending their children between times.

From this particular base, Johnny and I headed out on a 130-kilometre trip bound for the vast expanse of a salt lake where we would carry out a sun observation to fix a photo point for our map compilation. We hadn't had anything to eat all day and our work made us feel so peckish that when a bush turkey "attacked" us in the afternoon we proved the accuracy of the sights on our rifle. With the huge bird wrapped tightly in a canvas camp-sheet to keep away the blowflies, we carried on until after dark hoping to reach Kingoonya that night. To make the trip more quickly we tried a shortcut across a narrow neck of the salt lake to save skirting around it in a thirty-kilometre loop. This turned out to be one of the experiences which taught us forever after to treat such lakes like the plague. Halfway across, the surface broke and the going became heavy. We decided to reverse out of it but found it was already far too late as the jeep settled down with its underside locked firmly in the salt crust.

108

Four hours later with axes, shovels, and lifting jacks coated thickly with blue, salty mud, and dozens of chopped lengths of mulga trees arranged in a herring-bone corduroy roadway, we managed to drive the unfortunate little vehicle with its sad, deflated tyres the ten paces back to the hard bank. During this operation we discovered that a stick had put a small hole in the radiator hosing and in the effort of going even that short distance at high revs, the dry engine block heated to the point of stopping everything abruptly. Our cans of water had already gone into the radiator with each fruitless attempt to get out and we were by now feeling weak from hunger, the time being three o'clock in the morning.

Simultaneously our thoughts turned to the turkey in the camp-sheet so while we waited for the engine to cool, out it came and was soon cooking on a mulga fire, which also dried off our coating of wet mud. We didn't think much of our "shortcut" scheme as we walked out on to the salt pan with a shovel to dig a hole which would soon fill with brine seepage. We dipped pieces of the turkey in the brine, as a substitute for the salt shaker we didn't have, not planning to be away for so long.

After we had devoured our meal, it was necessary to fill the radiator; we had already temporarily bound the hole over with tape. Of course the only liquid available was the extremely salty water from the hole in the lake, and we were soon on our way, ready to replace this most corrosive engine-cooling arrangement with fresh water as soon as we arrived back. We reached the rail crossing near our base by six o'clock in the morning, and as if to cap off the evening's events, for the first and only time ever, we had to wait for a goods train bound for Perth to slowly pass by. It was mid-July so we were all but frozen solid as we reached our camp in the dead-finish bushes and lit a huge fire.

Several days later half our party was at East Well, with the other half including Harold left behind in Kingoonya. My old jeep had refused to go any further. The following day the mail train was due in with some parts we needed, and with the other vehicles also temporarily immobilised,

109

little Don and I planned to ride two of Joe's horses the forty-kilometre return trip to Coondambo. The journey took most of the day and for several days afterwards it was a case of "mantelpiece teas" for me, as Joe put it. If you couldn't sit down for meals, he reasoned, then you ate off the mantelpiece.

On the ride both horses slipped a shoe, so that involved a morning's blacksmithing for me in the outstation's work shed. I had learned to make horseshoes and to shoe horses while I was still at school, when I spent many hours at the end of the day watching and helping a blacksmith near by. No shoeing iron was available on the outstation so the new shoes were made of two old worn-out ones welded together on the anvil, with the thicker heels of one at the worn clip end of the other. I had seen my old blacksmith friend doing that so often that I could do it myself, much to the elation of my audience of Aboriginal stockmen.

It was at the main homestead that I first met old Mick Kelly, the man who told me the story of John Henry Davies' grave. Mick had worked for two bosses in his life, one on Arcoona and the other on Coondambo, after he came out to Australia from the United Kingdom in the late 1850s, when he was just a boy. A quick calculation suggested that he was in his nineties at present, but no one, least of all Mick, knew for sure. His first question to me, after noticing my huge hobnailed boots with only two holes tied up and no socks, was to ask if my boots pinched me. For several years until he died, his first greeting to me whenever I called in was always "Does yer boots pinch?"

Our stay at East Well, in between survey work, was spent learning the details of lamb tailing, Mules operations, stockwhip cracking, and helping Don with his radio correspondence school arithmetic problems. The Mules operation, we discovered, was the process of cutting two great boomerang-shaped pieces of skin from the rear end of the lambs. When healed, a wrinkle-free, drum-tight skin was formed, thus reducing the chances of blowfly strike. With no folds where flies could deposit their worms, the grown sheep would forever be safe, but at the time the

110

little lambs would run off to their mothers, stubs of tails and Mules gashes pouring out blood. The art of biting off the male lambs' testicles with our teeth in order to produce wethers had to be tried to complete our education of course, but after mastering it we were quite content to leave that part to Joe and the Aboriginal stockmen.

Then came the unforgettable day when we had our visitors, the most "different" from any we had encountered so far; even for the Australian outback they were unique. Luckily it was on a day I had reserved to be in the camp for calculations. As I was working I vaguely heard a commotion slowly growing louder. When the noise of dogs and trace chains sounded very close by, I closed the book of logarithms and went out of the shearers' hut office to investigate.

I couldn't believe my eyes at the unheralded group pulling into our camp. A woman was sitting on the cabin roof of an old Chevrolet truck, plying a whip to encourage the pair of camels pulling it along to keep moving through the fence, and yelling in a language only camels might understand. The swindle bar and chains just in front of where the engine would normally be located had there been one, were lying in the dust as the old truck rolled on after the camels decided to stop dead in their tracks. The back of this truck was heaped up with everything possible, from drums of water and wire to shovels and canvas rolls, while hurricane lamps, frying pans, and billies dangled in every available space around the load. An old armchair, wired into place, rode on top of the lot, and in it a shaggy dog covered in flies slept through it all. An old cart was hooked on behind, equally laden under which a dozen dogs stood or lay in the shade, and I wondered how two camels could possibly move it all along.

Arrayed round the procession was an escort of scraggy horses who barely supported the weight of the bushmen in their saddles and when I went over to greet them all, I noticed the cabin of the Chev was also crammed full of people, who spilled out on to the ground as soon as the wire loop holding the door shut was released.

George already had the water boiling and came over to inform the assembly, who were soon all sitting down around our eating bench in the shearers' kitchen.

Len Beadell
May '66

12

The First Plunge

into the Unknown

It wasn't long before we were joined by Joe who came
over from the homestead and welcomed the new arrivals
like long-lost cousins. He had known them for a great
many years on various sheep and cattle stations spread
over thousands of square kilometres, for they were dam-
sinkers travelling around the bush making earth dams as
requested for the catchment of what little rain fell. They
were wonderful people quite akin to the legendary folk to
be found in the hills of Kentucky, and although they were
a family apart from usual convention, they were experts in
their field. Their dams were built with the laborious
method of using horse-drawn scoops which would move
only a teaspoon of dirt at a time compared to later bulldozers and carryalls, but after months of beaverlike work, a
perfectly rectangular, deep hole was the result. Dug out
with an eye to topography, the future rains would all be
diverted into it, providing good water for stock during the
dry years.

They had decided to visit East Well on their slow,
lumbering way to their next assignment and as the whole

family tribe travelled everywhere together, the move was something to see. We had been increasingly interested in the fine art of stockwhip cracking and on noticing their collection, we brought up the subject. In no time, there and then, the wild younger members had their whips out and began giving us a demonstration. I was asked to hold up a small leaf in my fingers (which I must admit were those of my left hand, as I work with my right) and in a second, a whiplash exploded on the leaf leaving only half of it protruding from my finger and thumb. As if this weren't spectacular enough, a second whiplash followed with a gunshot impact, and half of what was left disappeared as well, to the lively yells of the visitors who had seen it all many times before. I dropped the tiny piece of leaf before a possible third attack was made.

They then proceeded to go through their repertoire. The "Sydney Flash" came next with one explosion in front of the boy plying the whip followed a split second later by another behind him and a final report out in front. Joe explained that another name for this exhibition was "Cow, horse, calf", because it is used when droving a cow and her calf while on horseback. The first crack got the cow moving while the second behind kept the drover's horse up with her, the last being reserved for the lagging calf. Imaginary snakes in the dust were chopped to pieces, and for the finale one boy cracked the lash around his own neck, finishing up with many coils of the thong around his throat.

This all started off a session of intense study. They trained us daily until they left, when Joe, who was good himself, carried on. I was always wary of cracking pieces of grass out of people's mouths, but in the bush everyone tries everything. For the following year, Joe's borrowed stockwhip became part of our gear, accompanying me with my theodolite wherever I went.

The dam-sinkers all slept on the dust under the wagon, varying the number of old blankets they pulled up around their ears with the current temperatures, fully clothed in riding gear and boots, with worn hats full of rags for a pillow.

Old Mick Kelly, who thought he came to Australia from the United Kingdom somewhere around the 1850s

Eventually they hitched their camels up to their "two-camelpower" truck, and with the mother sitting on the roof holding the lines from the animals' nose-pegs, with granny and some smaller babies wired back into the cabin, they pulled out of our camp amid a cloud of dust, the scraggy dog asleep once more on the armchair.

One night early in August while helping young Don with twenty-four sums the teacher had set him over the radio transceiver, the party line telephone rang and Joe went to answer it. Apparently a geologist, who with his field assistant had been carrying out a study of the rocks in the area partly on behalf of the Woomera project, was having trouble with his Mines Department truck and had walked to a boundary rider's hut he'd seen during that day. He'd found an old telephone nailed to a mulga post forming part of the wall, and by means of this managed to rouse up East Well. We enquired where he was and when he said he didn't know the name of the area, we asked him to go out of the hut and describe to us what he saw. Back came the answer that apart from a date palm growing alongside a headless windmill stand and a rusted-out stock tank, he couldn't see much else in the dark. That was enough to tell us exactly where he was, about fifty kilometres away on a far corner of the station, so we instructed him to sit tight and said we would come for him straight away. He thought the truck had a broken axle or transmission, and before ringing off he introduced himself as Tom Barnes from Adelaide. We packed away the homework books and set out in my jeep; it was only ten o'clock at night.

After a freezing drive, taking all the shortcuts we knew through the bush and steering by the stars when off the station tracks, Joe, Max, Don, and I finally arrived at the boundary rider's shed after midnight. Our headlights were trained on it, and Tom emerged and came over. The next thing was to find his truck in the scrub where he had left it with the assistant huddled in the cabin. This job took another hour in the pitch-black mulga, but we were helped by the assistant who switched on the headlights of the stranded vehicle when he heard our crashing approach. The

Top: Blue and Ron Stanford decided that Joseph Brooks built his trig cairn on the Knoll to last. This cairn was erected in 1875. *Bottom:* When Brooks couldn't find any stones, he often used mulga wood instead. Sometimes the wood had to be carted by dray for many kilometres. This example, trig station Hume, was sited near Twins homestead

offside rear wheel lay at a bad angle indicating a broken axle. That meant a towing job, only possible by making a 100-kilometre detour on the harder, more used motor tracks.

Frequently throughout that nightmare journey with Tom and his helper steering their crippled vehicle in a cloud of dust from the jeep, they would blink their headlights for us to stop as the back wheel brakes were once again on fire. Each time shovelled sand and a cooling spell were needed before we could resume this midnight trek which eventually brought us back to East Well just before the first evidence of the rising sun appeared in the sky.

As the next train from the west was due at midday, and would be needed if our bush mechanics couldn't repair the vehicle, we began dismantling the affected parts as soon as we pulled up. We'd driven 160 kilometres since interrupting Don's homework, but that wasn't even thought of as we lay under Tom's truck with handfuls of spanners. By mid-morning it became clear that it was a job for a workshop with hydraulic presses and spare parts, so as Tom made a separate parcel of his urgently-needed equipment both personal and geological, we arranged to drive him into Coondambo to catch the train to Adelaide. There he would start afresh with a sound vehicle, leaving the original one for us to drag into the siding for dispatch south on a goods train.

Tom Barnes was to become a lifelong friend, working with us on future projects all over South Australia, including geological work connected with the first atomic bomb tests held in Australia six years later. Soon after this association began he was elevated to the rank of Director of the State Mines Department.

Some more detailed work was required on the actual rocket launching site by now, involving many nights' camping alongside our rock pile near Ashton Hill to carry out astronomical observations. Rolling up my old swag and some tins of stew, George's bread, and plum jam, I went to live temporarily on the open gibber plains at a spot where nothing broke the horizon for the full circle. As it later

116

turned out, this site was abandoned owing to its proximity to another short or interim range which was to be used for initial testing of smaller missiles. After each night's star observation, a volume of calculations resulted which I worked out sitting on my bed roll in what must have been the most spacious air-conditioned office in the world.

All this time an expedition was being planned in Adelaide to discover what lay ahead for 400 kilometres in the direction of the centre-line of the rocket range. As I was included in the party, word came to our camp outlining the general aims. The trip was being planned in conjunction with General Evetts' office in England and it was to be the first such venture into the unknown from Woomera. For the first 300 kilometres, half-a-dozen sheep stations occupied the area but beyond that no one, not even the station owners, had penetrated the dense wall of mulga scrub which suddenly replaced the open saltbush plains west of the main Alice Springs road. Many star observations would be needed with results calculated on the spot to establish tentative future instrumentation points to track the behaviour of the missiles, and much sheer hard work, bushmanship, and hard living would necessarily accompany such a trip. I did not have much preparing to do as my life had consisted of just this for a long time, so with theodolite, tripod, stop watches, almanacs, and calculation tables, and with the inevitable canvas swag roll to hand, I was all set to head off at a moment's notice.

The army barracks in Adelaide had already been contacted for assistance with vehicles and supplies for the party and the task of assembling men and equipment was placed in the hands of their regimental sergeant-major, Gordon Burdon, an extremely capable old soldier whose entire life had revolved around the army. He was later the one man selected in the State to regularly lead the Colour Party in the Anzac Day march through Adelaide, and was still going twenty-six years later.

Shortly after we first heard of this development, a convoy of nine army trucks and jeeps pulled into our hillbillies' camp at East Well and parked with military precision in a perfect line by the woolshed. This was where I would begin as guide and surveyor, and within an hour we were on our way and old Joe and his family joined the camp members to farewell us out of the sliprails.

The first night away we all camped out in the mulga not far from our Kingoonya dead-finish bush camp, and as if to toughen up the new arrivals quickly, the sky opened with torrents of rain, driven by a howling wind. Although this made the group slosh about all night rolling up blankets and huddling in and under vehicles, the boys were a lot less disenchanted than I thought they'd be when morning came. After the clouds went, the temperature was just above freezing point, but the army cook still had an early breakfast ready for us before we hit the trail again.

An airfield built and used by the Department of Civil Aviation was located at Mount Eba Station, 100 kilometres north of Kingoonya. Very early in the planning it was thought that a rocket range head might be established there but the fact that this would involve ten times more rail than the site at Pimba would need, coupled with the additional 300-kilometre return trip from Adelaide, decided all involved against using it. It would also shorten the range length by 100 kilometres. Mount Eba was a normal stopping-off place for the regular flights from Darwin and Alice Springs to Adelaide, and an air reconnaissance plane had been organised to land there for us. The scientific party would fly up in it and would join the overland party after the inspection from the air.

Gordon Burdon marshalled his troops in an orderly fashion on our arrival at Mount Eba. The Dakota aeroplane landed on schedule that same day, bringing Group Captain Bill Dale, my old friend Major Wynne-Williams in his riding jodhpurs and socks, and a British artilleryman, Colonel John Caddy. The future chief scientist for the whole project, Alan Butement, and Group Captain George Pither, accompanied by an engineer by the name of Gray, made up the party and we immediately huddled over the few available maps covering our field of operations. This was to be an historic conference: we were the first group to forge ahead of the now rapidly expanding scene around the old Phillip Ponds area constantly referred to now as just plain "Woomera".

The outcome of our talks was that we would take off at first light next morning and fly on a compass course along my computed bearing of the centre-line. We'd see for ourselves what was in store for us beyond the last of the civilisation in that direction.

On the outward flight I was allowed the prime seat in the co-pilot's cockpit where I could set the compass by the results of my astronomical work at Marsella, seemingly done so long before. As we flew, the country below proved itself to be quite as devoid of life as we'd imagined. Beyond Mabel Creek homestead, the last of the occupied areas, the mulga belt stretched to the horizon. After much low-level circling in the air turbulence we returned to Mount Eba for lunch, having skipped over 800 kilometres.

The first and last time I had been in a plane was over the New Guinea jungles in the second World War, with more headhunters than soldiers making up the passenger list. I was so unused to this means of travel that it took me weeks to get over it. I had relinquished my cockpit seat to the co-pilot for the return, and on the Eba dirt strip I all but fell out of the door, proving that one has to be a stable airman to ride unaffected in the fuselage. John Caddy and the others casually read a book after the inspection was over while I lay in agony on the floor clutching a re-inforced brown paper receptacle—thoughtfully provided by the air force.

Alan Butement, being so expert with radio equipment, had each of the four jeeps fitted with intercom sets so that we could not only chat to each other but also to the pilot of the light Auster two-seater plane attached to our group. One army radio mechanic who was fresh out of training school confided to me that in effect Mr Butement knew nothing, and then proceeded to explain to him some complicated technical detail of the layout in the present transceiver circuit. Alan heard him out politely and the

119

army boy gave me a smug look of satisfaction. This some-how faded in the next few seconds as Alan Butement informed him that he himself had designed that particular feature in England in 1935.

Bob Crombie, who was manager of Mount Eba Station, invited us all into his homestead that night and Flo, his wife, produced a square linen tablecloth and asked the unique gathering to sign it in pencil. This started a ritual which was repeated with the arrival of every famous person to follow in the next fifteen years, and each time she would meticulously sew over the names in coloured silk thread. This tablecloth became legendary, eventually crammed with names embroidered in all the colours avail-able from the Young and Gordon station store in Kingoonya. It later included several pencil sketches I had added of the first helicopter to land at Eba and rockets with their crews, and the names of teams of scientists. Appearing on the cloth were kings, queens, governors-general, prime ministers, and world-famed atomic scientists who arrived on the Eba airstrip or came overland, mainly in connection with the Woomera Rocket Range. After the Crombies moved to Morapoi, a cattle and sheep station of their own near Kalgoorlie in Western Australia, I still ask to view this priceless cloth which Flo guards with her life twenty-five years later.

Next morning we all slowly pulled out of Eba to continue our overland journey of exploration, with each vehicle precisely eighty metres apart, in accordance with the army regulation. Under the eagle eye of Gordon Burdon everyone was made to stop to check tyres. This was all vastly different from our little survey camp at East Well; being a resident hillbilly I freelanced at will, but when I was with the rest of the party I complied with the rules to help set an example.

We all camped in the open at a station windmill and dam named the Penrhyn that night, and it proved to be a gigantic test of how everyone would stand the con-ditions. Black clouds rolled up and rain came down in sheets illuminated occasionally by flashes of forked lightning preceding explosions of thunder. Gale-force wind added to the turmoil, and altogether it was a sorry collection of people next morning, wringing water from blankets in the peaceful, sunny saltbush flat by the dam. This was my normal life, with nothing unusual about the night's events to make me comment, but at the same time I was elated to see how well everyone took it, with good humour and jokes by far outnumbering any scowls.

The army cook, as always, had the meal ready after using a can of petrol to start his fire, and the boys did all they could to help him. Several days before, he had chastised one man who had made a remark out of place regarding the size of his helping, and the tirade had frightened a flock of Bob Crombie's sheep, 800 metres away at the woolshed. This, coupled with the prize-wrestler build of the cook, caused all and sundry to respect him.

Eventually we were on the way again and I had the jodhpured Major Wynne-Williams with me as passenger. He chatted nonstop with the other vehicles over the intercom, describing everything as we were in the lead. The code name for my jeep set was "Dog", and Alan Butement was stuck with "Horace", so each conversation opened with "Dog to Horace, over". The reply would come back "Horace to Dog, over" until one day Alan demanded "Who called me Horace?" as he threw down his microphone. We gathered he wasn't completely in agreement with the choice of his code name which was forthwith changed to Henry. I shuddered when this brought back to mind the incident of the near-cremation in Frank Owen's camp at the Ponds.

We called into the next station, named Ingomar and occupied by Dick Rankin. Further tea and scones were enjoyed by our little party comprising the air reconnaissance group. The main convoy was marshalled and attended to by Gordon a kilometre away, so as not to disturb the usual peace and quiet of the homestead, a very thoughtful gesture.

Dick Rankin had come into this country many years

before and happened to be able to gain ownership of Ingomar Station, which eventually led to his acquisition of four more in the area, so his sons could all have one each and there were a couple to spare. A quiet, beautifully-spoken bushman, he accepted the evil-looking bottle of liquid the Englishmen offered him, after they told him they'd brought it all the way from Scotland. He informed me later he didn't know what to do with it as he didn't drink. Our work so often took me to his country that our association grew over the succeeding years, until he took up residence in Adelaide twenty years later and left the stations to his sons and managers. I suspect many trips followed his temporary retirement as his roots in that area lay very deep.

Eventually we struggled into the opal fields of Coober Pedy which we'd heard so much about from our transitory visitors at the Ponds and I enquired about some of them. One was still there and showed me the very car which still had the penny I'd soldered over the hole in the petrol tank earlier in the year. The convoy clustered around, similar to a wagon train in Arizona's Wild West, on the saltbush "prairies" ten kilometres from the settlement while we made our inspection. As in Andamooka, everyone lived in holes in the ground. I asked George Morousen, an old Afghan who carted their wood on a draught-horse-drawn buckboard from a mulga patch fifty kilometres away, why it was called Coober Pedy. He told me that long ago that "Coober" meant white man in Aboriginal language and "Pedy" was their word for a dug-out hole. Thus Coober Pedy meant "White fella dig out". In those days the only above-ground structure was the Young and Russell store shed, Jack Young being a relation of one of the owners of the Young and Gordon's stores at Port Augusta and Kingoonya.

This country was full of interest, we thought, as we attempted to contact anyone about, by peering into the assortment of caves one by one.

13

Beyond the Last Habitation

I have always considered we were fortunate to have first happened on the cave occupied by the Wilson family. Jack Wilson, from Cornwall, was most knowledgeable, not only about opals and opal-cutting, but most worldly subjects which could be brought up. He and Major Wynne-Williams had many long conversational battles regarding the merits of Wales over Cornwall and vice versa. He was in the process of building an above-ground dwelling at the site of a newly-discovered patch of opal known as "The Eight Mile", but our meeting in his dug-out home proved unforgettable. Their beds were on the floors of extra holes dug into the walls, as were clocks, tins of food, and everything else, so they took up no further space in the main excavation; above the pillow end of the beds were squares of material nailed to the dirt roof to prevent particles of the clay from dropping into the sleepers' eyes. A hole dug to the surface over the stove gave ventilation. Mrs Wilson had recently been to the army surplus sales in Alice Springs where she bought an old three-ton blitz buggy and drove it the 800 kilometres back to Coober Pedy single-handed, mending broken fan belts and attending to mishaps on the way. She later rolled another over in the desert and left it there.

Of course the brief pause at the fields had to include a venture down an opal hole where George Pither dug diligently with a pick for an hour until he surfaced displaying a miscroscopic piece of coloured potch. His air force colleague, Bill Dale, declined the offer to submerge himself in the dusty cavity, and stayed above ground advising all and sundry that a group captain was below possibly gouging out a precious gemstone. He thought it was unusual that a man of such an exalted rank should be doing such a thing.

That day our little aeroplane landed on the road near by. Arrangements were made for Flight Lieutenant Pilot Pete, if and when requested, to drop things to our small party when we left the main convoy on the highway and pushed ahead into the mulga to the north-west. With that we packed up and moved off to form a base at a bore fourteen kilometres north of Mabel Creek homestead, fifty kilometres away. We would operate from that camp on the first overland attempt to reach a point, pre-plotted on the blank map, labelled the "250 Mile O.P." With my astronomical observations we hoped to arrive at a point which would plot on this location, with a view to a future rocket tracking station. It was never used for such an operation, as more sophisticated equipment was developed, but at that time it was a proposed part in the planning stages of Woomera.

Mabel Creek was occupied by an old bushman called Alf Turner, who owned thousands of square kilometres of country but only had three water bores on his place. He roamed all over the north-west for many years until he finally settled on Mabel Creek where he lived in a galvanised-iron shed. His one faithful white station hand was Don Tanner who had come into the bush from Adelaide at the age of thirteen and had stayed there ever since. When Mabel Creek later changed hands to Ken Neil, and then Dick Rankin, and finally to Dick's son, Ian, Don Tanner went with it as part of the deal. Many years later he married, and they opened up their own schoolhouse sporting a Government teacher for his half-dozen or so children and those of Ian.

Alf wasn't as interested in his station as he was in the bottles of bush brew made for him by his partner's mother who also lived there. Dick Hann and his mother had joined him in acquiring the station and she looked after the cooking in the tin shed, which would very often rock to its foundations as an occasional bottle of "awkward stuff" would explode with the force of a stick of gelignite. Rip-roaring cyclonic gales would batter Mabel Creek constantly and to this day, whenever I think of wind, I think of that hut on the plains where we arrived on this historic first trek.

With a view to seeing what sort of country lay beyond their western boundary, which was vaguely defined as being twenty kilometres away in the bush, it was decided to have Dick accompany us on the main part of the trip to the 250 Mile O.P. The night before we were to push on Colonel John Caddy took out his beautiful, silver-inlaid century-old shotgun and asked me if I would accompany him on a turkey shoot, hoping Alf wouldn't think he was poaching.

I told him Alf didn't even know of the English country-side laws and wouldn't mind at all, but emphasised that only several of these birds were to be seen a year, if you were lucky. Undaunted, off he set along the dry bed of the Woorong Creek which joined Mabel Creek, with me following quietly, not wanting to disturb any possible game. I told him the fowl were protected and it was illegal to touch them unless it was a case of life or death for a starving bushman, but he thought this occasion was just that. As dusk crept on we returned to camp. John announced to the cheering gathering that although he didn't actually bag a turkey, the shot everyone must have heard at least brought results, and he held up the mutilated body of a poor rabbit for all to see.

After two days in which I tried in vain to secure a star

latitude and longitude observation through the clouds, we decided to forge on, hoping the skies would clear later. I had luckily gained a latitude result from the sun, which would help us return by compass to the camp at the bore. Our reconnaissance party with Dick Hann headed off after I plotted a compass bearing, helped by the sun observation.

The mulga became very dense, and dry scrub from blown-over dead trees staked our tyres as we pushed the jeeps to their limits with the "Dog to Henry" conversations running nonstop. Some low sand ridges began to appear in the thick bush, and by nightfall we had travelled sixty-eight kilometres according to our speedos.

John Caddy's jeep began to have petrol trouble in the late afternoon and it persisted until we camped to fix it. The fault turned out to be a small beetle jammed in the fuel line at the pump. During the day the clouds began dispersing and the sky was mostly clear, so I set up my theodolite away from the glare and shimmer of their enormous fire and began to observe. Alan Butement was most excited and impressed with all this, as were the others. After several hours spent waiting for breaks in the clouds I managed to see enough stars to obtain a position. We spread out a canvas camp-sheet nearer the warm fire and as torches were shone on my old calculation book, I began the sums. All else was forgotten during this operation. When each step was completed, Alan would start to leap up, thinking we had a result. He was dying to plot our position on the map spread out ready on the bonnet of a jeep, but each time I had to restrain him and tell him I hadn't quite arrived at the answer yet.

At long last I drew a line under a set of figures and announced that these were actually the latitude and longitude of the spot where we were camping. Alan flew to the open map and scaled off the values, finishing up with a pencil cross on the bare sheet. His next exuberant remark was to be used by us for ever after at the conclusion of the many astrofixes which followed. His excited English accent rang out in the otherwise quiet bush, penetrating

126

the blackness beyond the firelight, "By Jove I say! But isn't it fun finding out where you are?"

This position showed us to be thirty-eight kilometres south-east of our goal. Next morning, in the gloom thrown over the heavy bush by the reappearance of the black cloud coverage, we carried on. Driving through the feature-less mulga scrub on full-cloud days makes it almost im-possible to hold a straight-axis course so keeping it clear of the jeep's magnetic attraction, I paid a lot of attention to my prismatic compass, reading out my plotted bearing. That morning the little Auster plane buzzed us after locating the vehicles by means of our radio chat-back, but to this day I don't know why. He couldn't land, didn't need to drop anything, and couldn't see far in the clouds under which he was flying, and even if he could, there was absolutely nothing to see.

Our aim was to arrive at a fictitious point on a blank map, 400 kilometres along the centre-line of the range and nineteen kilometres off it to the north. By mid-afternoon I announced that we were as close as possible by dead reckoning from the last night's star fix to the 250 Mile O.P., so we grouped the jeeps into a square and the party rolled out their swags. The usual enormous British-style fire was built, too hot to stand near or cook on and using up all the dry wood within a large radius, but at least it looked cheerful. Everyone was a little glum because the clouds seemed bent on preventing any more star work, but I set up my theodolite once more clear of the fire's shimmer and laid out the books and stop watches on my swag of blankets, just in case.

After our meal of fried bully-beef, the discussions around the fire led to enquiries about Australian bush lore. One asked why it was called "bully-beef", which Alan quickly answered with his theory that it was beef cut straight off a bull. Being an electronics pioneer he was asked how the bats constantly whizzing past our ears did so without colliding with anything. That produced a long explanation of how radar impulses emitted by the bats returned impulses from near-by objects, automatically guiding the little blind creatures clear of crashes. Just then one flicked past John Caddy's face and he confidently didn't move a muscle, informing everyone "There goes one of those bats equipped with its little radar set."

I had gathered some wild peaches or quandongs during the day, so I produced some and offered one to Wynne-Williams who gave the mumbled opinion that they were pretty tart. Alan, having only heard the last part of the comment, sprang to his feet and probed the circle of bush outside the glow of the fire with eyes shielded by his hand, and asked "Where is this pretty tart?" He certainly had the lively sense of humour given only to those who feel at home anywhere regardless of whether conditions are good or bad. Over a great many years on the occasional expeditions which he and I later made together I never found him otherwise.

One by one the assembly grew tired, rolling themselves in their blankets by the fire, soon to be sound asleep. John was last and came over to me to commiserate over the lack of stars for a fix. Just as he lay down in his swag, one bright planet showed itself vertically overhead through a small gap in the clouds. He leapt up, grabbed me by the shoulder, and pointing skywards, shouted "I say, Beadell! What about that one?" Before I could explain to him that its position in the sky could not be used for an observation of any kind, it vanished as quickly as it had appeared. Back he crawled into his swag and I sat there alone by the fire listening to the heavy breathing and occasional snores coming from the exhausted scientists scattered about among the clumps of saltbush.

Eventually I lay down in my canvas roll alongside my theodolite away from the fire, as there didn't seem any sign of the clouds dispersing, and I must have been asleep within seconds.

This was not to be for long, I realised, when something caused me to wake and look at the sky; the importance of the work must have been implanted in my mind. As I sleepily peeped out from my blankets I'm not sure if I felt glad or sorry when I discovered that there above was a clear sky with an unobstructed dome of bright stars shining down on me. At first I couldn't believe it but then as the blanket slipped away from my eyes, buried once more, there it was again with the silhouette of the theodolite tripod beckoning me. My watch showed me it was one o'clock. After a short inner battle with myself, I sat up, pulled my hobnailed boots from their location under some rags serving as a pillow, and opened the theodolite box where I'd replaced the instrument before turning in.

In minutes I was so engrossed with star observing that I forgot all about the cold numbing my fingers and didn't stop until I'd carried out a complete position-line fix using eight stars, entering the results on the dewy pages of my old field book. When I had received the radio time signal which gave me the precise error of the chronometer at the instant of the observations, I packed away the instrument after wiping off the droplets of my breath which had condensed on the cold brass as I worked, and took down the tripod. All the valuable results, which I'd work out later, were then safely placed in the box of calculation books. At last, much more contentedly, I was able to crawl back between the blankets. This whole operation went unnoticed by the party whose heavy breathing still radiated into the cold air from their positions around the heap of white ashes left by the camp-fire. I knew that if the protective blanket of ash was disturbed it would reveal friendly, warm, red coals. It was a temptation to go over and poke some dry sticks of mulga into them to relieve the numbness of my fingers which had been held up to the screws of the theodolite for the previous few hours, open to the freezing night air. Tiredness won the contest and I once again adopted the horizontal position of the others for what was left of the night.

The first scene on which I focused in the grey morning, cloudy again, was the mulga trees glowing in the cheery blaze from the fire, with the dark shape of Alan, hands on hips and thumbs out in front as usual, pacing around my bed roll. Immediately he noticed that I had at last opened my eyes, he voiced his sadness that the incessant clouds had made us miss out on this most sought-after astrofix. To put him and the rest of the party out of their misery I threw back the blankets and led him over to the fire where I made an announcement.

It was amazing the effect that my news of the evening's events had on everyone; they jumped about, rubbing their hands and mumbling something about their doubts regarding Australian bushmen being dispelled forever. The success of the first exploratory expedition along the centre-line of the new rocket range now being assured, we ate some more fried slabs of bully-beef and painted a small, blackened piece of wood with the words "250 Mile O.P." This was nailed to a mulga peg I had chopped with my axe, and a photograph was taken of everyone assembled round the astronomical station.

This was our turning point for the present trip and we headed south-east for our main camp at the bore, not retracing the wheeltracks we made on our way out. These of course followed a weaving pattern from the results of the sun observations and previous star fix to this last goal. We managed to cover the whole distance to the army boys during that day. As the clouds had left us for good by mid-morning, on the way we took another sun observation to check our direction. Group Captain Bill Dale wore his collar and tie throughout and it is certain that this was the first occasion on record since Australia's discovery that such a thing has happened. To get out of a swag roll on a saltbush flat and put on a tie was completely unheard of, but rigid habits die hard with some, and at least it would have been handy as a ready ligature in case of snakebite.

No sooner had we rejoined Gordon Burdon and his men than I prepared for another astronomical observation to be done that same night on a hill near Mabel Creek home-stead, where I had arranged for a bush-wood beacon to be built while we were away. Bill Dale accompanied me on the fourteen-kilometre drive after tea to help me with booking the results, and once again it was two o'clock in the morning before we were back at the bore for a sleep which could only last a few hours. I mused that at this rate I

Top: The replacement engine flown up for the stranded passenger plane at Mount Eba. It seemed to be attached by surprisingly few flimsy bolts. *Bottom:* Molly and Angelene felt much safer with their own slower means of transport

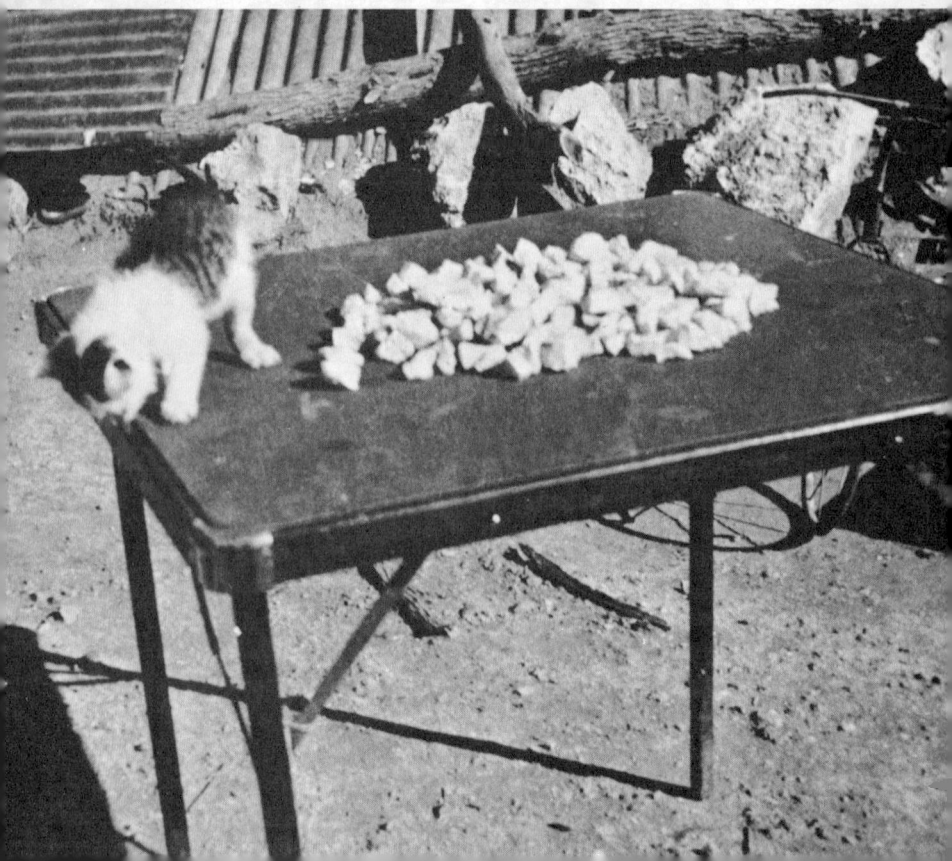

should be getting too tired to think, although I'd been used to night observations for so long that it wasn't yet having any effect. The enormity of the programme ahead by far outweighed any personal efforts put into it or any discomforts experienced, and I was grateful to be fit enough to cope with it.

That same morning we all pulled out and headed slowly back: "back" for them was Woomera, and for me East Well. Our camp at the Penrhyn was much less eventful than on the way out when we were drenched by the rain. Everyone formed a queue to take turns in viewing the moon through my theodolite telescope.

Next morning as the convoy followed, the vehicles exactly eighty metres apart, Bill Dale and I decided to press on faster to Mount Eba so that I would have a better chance of completing the calculations of my last two astrofixes. These results had to be taken south by an air force Dakota which would be landing there to whisk the battered scientists back to Adelaide for more conferences. The drive in the open jeep from the Penrhyn to Mount Eba was, to date, by far the worst I had ever found necessary to undertake.

Once again black clouds were with us by morning, followed by a deluge of rain which lasted for the rest of that day and night, making me wonder if this arid country ever really had a chance to become dusty. Added to this, a howling gale developed driving the heavy rain almost horizontally, and the temperature was as close to freezing as possible without turning the lakes of water over the wheeltracks of the main "road" into ice. Ours was an open-sided jeep with one piece of flat canvas for a roof which needn't have been there at all, and soon wasn't, as the roaring wind ripped it to shreds. The windscreen wiper was a manually-operated affair with a handle, so as I drove through the storm, I had one hand on the wheel and the other raised to the handle, working the arm back and forth in order to be able to dimly see the worst of the potential bog holes ahead. My old military overcoat fell away, baring my arm until it was purple with the cold. When the colour

Top: We made a new sign from a truck tail-board when the Wilsons bought the only store on the Coober Pedy opal field. *Bottom:* Bert Wilson's cat wasn't impressed by the £2,000 parcel of opal Bert had just bought from an Aboriginal gouger. "Pick out a stone for yourself—not too big though."

reached a certain hue I changed arms, and carried on like this for 140 kilometres until we arrived at Mount Eba homestead.

Flo Crombie was first to see us; as used as she was to seeing spent bushmen, the sight must have been well engraved on her mind for she has reminded me about that day ever afterwards. As soon as my arms returned to a more normal colour, Bill and I reluctantly left our places by her cooking stove and drove over to the shearers' meal shed. He got a fire going while I spread out my books and began the vital sums which would bring success to this inaugural expedition; I worked on into the night by the glow shed from an old kerosene lamp, long after Bill turned in to his swag in the kitchen.

I was fully rewarded by the satisfying way the star observations worked out, giving me the final latitude and longitude for the hill at Mabel Creek and the all-important 250 Mile O.P. Then I collapsed into my own blanket roll on the floor.

14

No Time to Waste Sleeping

The roar of an aeroplane's engines overhead woke me with a start and as I didn't have to dress in anything different from what I'd slept in, I was soon over on the airstrip to greet the pilots. Returning to the kitchen in my still wet and mud-caked jeep, they were able to report to their group captain and join us for a hot cup of tea.

During the afternoon the main party rolled in and, regimental to the last, lined up their bumper bars in an orderly fashion alongside the woolshed. Alan Butement was eager to see how the results had computed, so as soon as he leapt out of his jeep, he, George Pither, and the others rushed over and soon we were all huddled around the mess table as I showed them the exact plotted positions of where we had just been. Wynne-Williams had been trying to use a prismatic compass and speedo readings to plot the course we travelled, but had only used the instrument while sitting in the vehicle.

The magnetic attraction of all that close ironwork didn't help him but he persevered throughout. John Caddy remarked to me once, after one of the Major's plots looked feasible, that it would have been quite meritorious if he "had any faith at all in what Wynne was doing".

Armed with the figures and soggy, crumpled maps, most of the exploratory party climbed aboard the Dakota and were soon airborne, off to a more hospitable region with the little Auster in snail-like pursuit. Wynne stayed with the ground party, as did John Caddy, and we continued overland back home—wherever that might be.

There was another old survey mark of Brooks on the way which we thought could be a good site for the 50 Mile O.P., so after finding it and writing a description of the country around it, we camped on an open flat near Parakylia Station homestead. Parakylia was owned by Walter Greenfield and he was very anxious to hear of the outcome of the trip and the future regarding his station and the rockets. We assured him that it wouldn't make any difference to him and if anything, help could come of it in the planned village with its hospitals, shops, regular air services, and other amenities.

On the morning of the last day of this expedition we called into Roxby Downs, the station belonging to Walter's brother. Shearing happened to be in progress at the woolshed, giving Wynne and John an ideal chance to see what goes on. During our tour of inspection, one burly shearer thrust a shearing handpiece out, one hand holding the front leg of a struggling sheep, and shouted for me to "have a go". The following exhibition of this particular wool clip satisfied the audience as well as myself that there was more to this business than at first appeared. The sheep hated me and as the wool came off in anything but a complete fleece, I heard Wynne calling "Bravo!" above the general noise. John stood well back for fear he too might get an emergency haircut. The sweat-soaked shearer took over once again at his stand and immediately made the art of sheep shearing look the easiest thing a person could do.

Dave Greenfield, the owner, often referred to himself as a "Dinky Die Squatter", which in effect he was. Dave and Norman Greenfield from Purple Downs were cousins whose fathers came into this country fifty years before;

134

with Norman's brothers, Irwin and Colin, each owning stations, the Greenfields have very deep roots hereabouts.

That afternoon our little jeep slowly pulled into Woomera, thus closing another chapter in the initial history of the birth of the Australian rocket range. We had hurriedly passed by Yandandaree Ridge where I still vividly remembered eating those discs of double-sided sandpaper cooked in the sandstorm.

As if I hadn't had enough shearing for one day, two cooks stationed in our old Ponds' kitchen asked for a haircut "seeing as how I was on the spot", so out came my ever-ready clippers. One of these cooks had the most serious and really miserable expression I'd ever seen, with low, drooping brows and mouth down so far at the corners that the lines continued on under his chin. Of course his standard nickname was "Happy". After a long session of earbashing we set up camp for the night at the Ponds. Then we drove up to the escarpment where my aerodrome was now being used more frequently, to the waiting Dakota. It had of course reached there an hour after leaving Mount Eba and the bulk of the party had finalised their affairs while awaiting our overland arrival, after first indulging in a lengthy bathing session with water from the dam.

It wasn't long before all the members of our expedition, apart from me, climbed on to the plane after handshakes and slaps on shoulders indicating a satisfactory end to the trip, and took off in a cloud of red dust. Many conferences would result from this, attended by General Sir John Evetts, and the vague outlines of further operations would possibly be made clearer.

On schedule, Mick Waterland arrived in one of our own jeeps from East Well and together we drove back to our camp there. It was now time to pack up and move to another base more central to the work. The members of our little camp were naturally keen to hear about the journey and the first night back was filled with the stories of what lay ahead. Joe and Don Stanford were full of questions about the country to the north-west but at long last we climbed into our swags. For me this was the first time I had slept under a roof for many weeks.

Mount Eba was our next choice as a base and two days later we were all dragging ourselves slowly through Kingoonya and on to Bob and Flo Crombie's place. We'd mentioned to them only a week before that such a move was planned. Harold was first to pull out in order to have a longer stopover at Kingoonya, and by nightfall we had reached the station and were unloading all the cats, dogs, and kangaroo near the empty shearers' huts. George headed for the kitchen to see to the evening meal, but the station cook was already there and from that moment onward, as could be expected, the relationship between the two degenerated, until the day not long after when the station cook pulled out.

We had arranged for a sheep to be killed and hung, which George broke up and cooked piece by piece. After a span of several days Bob asked if we were ready for another, to be informed there was still plenty left. He was amazed and told us that a sheep lasted the usual cook only half that time. George replied in the full hearing of his colleague that he "carved" the meat and didn't "hack" it. That did it. When he was on his own he was approached and asked if he would also act as station cook on the side for an extra wage. Our George continued for two-and-a-half months in this capacity and we could be quite certain that the station never had it so good.

We decided to live in a couple of tents rather than use the shearers' quarters, and while they were being pitched, a haircutting session was in progress. I cut not only our own members' locks but those of Bob, the station stockmen, the bookkeeper, and old McGaskill who was employed to refuel the DCA aeroplanes. Nearly seventy, he had a pointed beard and often felt "crook". His standard saying was to the effect that he didn't see why he should ever die because he had never done so before.

No sooner had we all resumed our surveys than an urgent trip to Adelaide came into the picture and I had to head off in a jeep on the 800-kilometre trip to investigate this latest development in the rocket range. It had been nearly half a year since I last had to see such civilisation and I hoped it wasn't going to become a habit.

After I gleaned all the information necessary for future fieldwork, I had to go for a renewal test for my army driving licence. The official in polished boots told me to drive over a sandhill near the beach. It might have been more to the point to ask me if I could drive on bitumen roads.

Then, on entering a gun shop in Adelaide to collect a part for one of our rifles, I noticed some coiled-up stock-whips hanging on a rack, so I commented on them. The shop owner soon found out where I'd been and a breath of the outback came to the busy footpath outside when, at his request, I gave an impromptu demonstration of the Sydney Flash or Joe's "Cow, horse, calf" whipcracking. A crowd soon formed and one by one they held papers out to be clipped off and one little girl volunteered to stand and be flogged, with the whip encircling her waist after the gunshot sound exploded from the lash. The shopkeeper was delighted at the attention drawn to his establishment but we decided to cease operations at the sight of an approaching police car.

On my way back to the bush again next morning I felt free once more as the chains seemed to drop away behind me. After a meal at the Ponds, dinner at East Well, a mug of tea at Kingoonya, and camp at Mount Eba, I was ready to get back to work immediately.

I was there only one night before I was woken by Ozzie and Mick who had walked in from their broken-down truck fifteen kilometres away at the "nettin'", a vermin-proof netting fence of a style used for boundaries between stations. George cooked an early breakfast for the three of us and we drove back in my jeep to look into the trouble, for the truck held a load of perishable supplies from Kingoonya. Hours of tests and dismantling rewarded us with the knowledge that the distributor spindle had seized, shearing off the pin holding the oil-pump drive cog. From my container of ten-centimetre nails carried for pegging out kangaroo and fox skins on claypans, I was able to select one of the right thickness to replace the broken pin. The first operation of course was to hammer out the spindle from its casing and file the rough edges smooth enough to be able to replace it freely. We soon had the vehicle mobile and our rough bush job enabled us to get it back to the camp. It would have to be driven to Woomera for a complete new part and the expert attention which was now available there.

That trip couldn't be wasted so I carried out two more astrofixes and three sun observations on the way, for the latest developments which I had only just been made aware of in Adelaide. On our return in the newly-serviced truck we called in at Coondambo and took some supplies out to East Well, which saved Joe, his wife, and Don a day's trip in their horse-drawn buckboard. After cutting their hair, we pressed on.

Back at Eba, half a day was enough to pack up, then we headed north to fix some vital points. We were off again to the saltbush plains near Billa Kalina Station, owned by Colin Greenfield, brother of Norman and Irwin. From the homestead one could see nothing in any direction but stony plains and an occasional flat-topped hill. Colin's small son and daughter were eager to accompany us on our initial reconnaissance and we had to wait until Glenys had her hair combed and a ribbon tied in it. Her mother explained this had to be done as "You never know who you might run into". Real bush people certainly have a sharp and unique sense of humour to be found nowhere else in the world but in the Australian "back country".

Without returning the eighty kilometres to Eba, I decided to continue on to the south-easterly regions from Billa Kalina where more important work was needed. Soon I rolled out my swag on the one-time high-water level alongside the Devil's Playground. My uncomputed star observations near Colin's homestead remained safely in my field books and after the proposed two more nights' observing, I was getting the idea that I was accumulating a lot of office work to do back in my tent at Eba.

The Devil's Playground is a large, flat depression covered with cane grass, and after rain the expanse fills with water which can only be seen around the edges. There was still a quantity of water left by the previous year's flood and I was able to use this for washing and to fill the radiator. The sandhills to the east were dotted with circular claypans, 100 meters in diameter, and all dry. From a careful inspection of the air photos I detected that one in particular had a small creek spearing its circumference, and being the only one I could positively identify, it had to be located on the ground.

The cattle and sheep men found this a source for many jokes at my expense: a "stargazer" who had an aversion to each of the hundreds of claypans but one. To them they were all the same, seen every time they were mustering in that area. There followed a long search for *the* one, tracing out each valley between the ridges in the vicinity. After two days of laborious scrutiny I topped a ridge to begin again, when spread out before me was a claypan with the definite point of a watercourse lined with saltbush extending almost to its centre. This was it. I drove out across the hard, level clay to camp at the apex where I set up my theodolite and laid out the books and stop watches, chronometer, and radio receiver ready to use when darkness fell.

The aim of so many of these operations was to locate a definite point on the ground which corresponded with a needle-prick mark on the emulsion of an appropriate air photo taken at 7600 metres. This same point must appear on nine photographs altogether, three on each overlapping parallel run of the aeroplane's flight, and three on the cross runs. The results of the star latitude and longitude of such a point would then rigidly fix its exact geographical location on a huge map plot back in our survey head-quarters, enabling the final map to be drawn. Parties from our survey camp would follow out tracks and fence lines or anything else there, marking them in ink on the photo surface. This information would later be transferred to the final map and an up-to-date accurate plan of the whole area required would be the result, to be used, in this case, to design a rocket range with its instrumentation.

I had found a wild pie-melon during that day so for tea I had my first sample of a melon boiled in claypan water to which two handfuls of sugar had been added. If you didn't concentrate too much on the taste it could easily have resembled stewed apples.

Next morning's packing up proved very easy for nothing, however small, could be left behind as it would show on the "bedroom floor", smooth as a billiard table. Driving back westward to the rim of the Devil's Playground, I was soon on the station track from Billa Kalina to Walter's Parakylia homestead, near which lay the next point to be fixed, which we'd located on the O.P. expeditions. It was at Brooks' old trig survey mark called Reedy Lagoon, a name which totally belied the locality. I had dinner with Walter, and he fired a constant barrage of questions at me regarding the future of his station which lay on the centre-line of the range. He naturally envisaged a nonstop profusion of silver rockets with flames gushing out of their jets landing on and around his house, but I was able to set his active mind quite at rest.

Retracing the wheeltracks made by the last expedition, as we had returned through here from Eba, I again prepared for another night's observing, thinking that we never seemed to have much time for lying about sleeping. It proved an uncomfortable evening with the arrival of a stiff breeze, making it necessary to hold the pages of the open field books down with an assortment of hammers and plumb-bobs. This spot was a likely location for the 50 Mile O.P.

To complete the huge triangular trip back to Eba I searched for and discovered another one of Brooks' marks on Peephabie Cliff, a small rocky rise in a sea of saltbush. Then, without a road to guide me, I drove back across country to my camp. Almost immediately upon arrival I began the astronomical calculations to arrive at my results as soon as possible, so we could carry on with the enormous amount of work, which still had really only just begun.

For relaxation after two days of sums, we decided to go

140

for a drive, of all things, through the mulga scrub to obtain a kangaroo to be eaten by the members of a small Aboriginal camp near by. Two of the children, Jimmy and Janey Austin, accompanied us, and several station hands, Blue, Skeeter, and Henry, made up the party. By the time we returned with the kangaroo, we had mended two staked tyres, collected a .22 bullet-hole in the canvas roof of the jeep, and been successful in extinguishing a raging fire around the exhaust pipe under the vehicle. It had been extensive enough to ignite the weeping oil from the gearbox and transfer case as well; needless to say it wasn't my usual vehicle we used, which I was constantly clearing of herbage, and which didn't seem to have a canvas roof either. We kept urging Henry to unload his rifle between chases but with the bouncing of the butt end on the floor between his knees, the resulting neat hole in the roof indicated clearly that he hadn't listened. As I returned to my sums I wondered if in fact we had actually been rewarded with any relaxation after all.

A day later one of the most severe dust tornadoes we'd encountered so far in this country hit Mount Eba with violent lashings of dust and sand unleashed in full fury. Our tents were tested to their limits and the swags and gear were soon moulded with overburden, causing me to transfer my mathematical operations to the shearers' kitchen which George had battened down against the force of the wind. At the height of the storm I heard a banging on the door and young Jackie Blacksill almost fell inside. He had been out mustering on his horse when it had all started. After riding back to the station through the blinding dust, he first tended his horse at the yards and stable before staggering through the onslaught towards his quarters near the kitchen. He was only about sixteen and all that was visible were the whites of his eyes and pink tongue as he flopped down to drink the mug of tea George had ready.

Jackie, Henry, Skeeter, and Blue slept in a line of thick-walled rooms built of natural rock. Every morning without fail and well before dawn, the blare of their radios turned

141

up full blast reverberated through the air with the yodelling of the hillbilly, cowboy songs about droving on the
plains. Aeroplane refueller, old McGaskill, somehow put
up with it, but it was one of the reasons we decided to live
in our tents while at our base. Even then we couldn't help
but be entertained by the screamed story of the feud
between the Martins and the Coys, and the way an old
stockman lay dying, embellished by the barking of the
many sheepdogs which were roused and wholeheartedly
joined in.

As it happened, I was on the brink of a far worse
experience which was to begin, luckily coinciding with the
completion of my astro sums, one day later.

142

15

A Trip
to the Dentist

A second left mandibular molar, as it is scientifically called, when in the process of becoming abscessed is, according to its owner, the very worst fate that could ever befall him, outstripping by far the rack, thumbscrews, and fingernail extractions for sheer torture. There was no argument in my mind as to the validity of this when, as I was completing the records of the recent star observations, I felt a slight discomfort in my lower left back tooth. Thinking it would go shortly I went to inspect the wooden bucket of wattle bark brew in which a couple of kangaroo skins were steeped for tanning.

They were coming along nicely, I discovered, but I didn't fully concentrate on working them about in the red liquid as instructed by Joe Stanford six months before, as the nagging ache seemed to be growing. I spent a great deal of that night wandering about the bush, not being able to even lie down, let alone sleep, and by morning I wasn't even aware of the hillbilly session. Throughout the day I couldn't eat anything and the agony mounted by the minute until a swelling appeared on the outside of my jaw.

Nothing would ease the pain, not even ice from our little kerosene refrigerator, and as the evening drew on I was incapable of keeping still, tired though I was from all the recent, sleepless star nights. The nearest help of any kind was at Port Augusta, 480 kilometres away, involving a drive of that distance or a 100-kilometre jeep trip to Kingoonya where I might possibly climb on to one of the infrequent trains from the west for the rest of the journey.

This was one of several such incidents which much later caused me to enter a crash-course in dentistry at the Woomera Hospital given by the dentist at the time, Bruce Dunstan. I have seen others walking the sandhills night after night in their endeavours to escape the pain and my current predicament gave me personal understanding of just how much they were suffering. I now have twenty-nine notches on my forceps but at the time I didn't possess that knowledge in any shape or form.

Over the station's Flying Doctor transceiver, Bob ascertained that the next train from Kalgoorlie was due in another two days, so I tried to work out the time it would take me to drive all the way in my present delirious state. It seemed to be about the same but in any event I had to tackle the exit from Eba one way or another, or lie down and die on the spot.

The next night was probably the most torturous I can ever remember spending anywhere, especially so far removed from outside help. I certainly didn't have to worry about being disturbed in the morning by the yodelling cowboys as by then I was pacing up and down the airstrip emitting lots of groans of my own.

Then, to make matters worse, as I loaded up my open jeep with several jerrycans of petrol, intending to set off straight away without even a swag, it started to rain. The country, as I'd so often found out, becomes a quagmire in the wet, offering no assurance whatever of arriving any-where, but I couldn't think straight enough then to realise how this latest development added to my plight.

The rain deluged down all the afternoon and during that time Bob sloshed over to the camp with the news that an east-bound train was due in Kingoonya just after midnight. This information settled how I should travel, because by now the country was turning into a pattern of miniature rivulets. As soon as the last tin of petrol was installed I sat in the soaking jeep and headed off alone. The rain could have been brought by the recent cyclone-force winds which only days before had caused a dust storm. If I could have thought anything at all I might have repeated the phrase "What a country!" to myself.

That drive down to Kingoonya was the most nightmarish anyone could ever hope to embark upon, with the constant threat of hopeless bogs every metre of the way, and with excruciating pain in my abscessed jaw. The rain lashed down on me as I drove, unprotected by anything but an old overcoat, by then wringing with water and chilled by the wind, and my hobnailed boots were filled as the cold rain cascaded down my bare legs. I steered almost by instinct, not being able to see even as far as the headlight glow, and as each lake across the road came up I tensed for the ride through, half-wondering if that was where I'd be stopped for good in a deep bog hole.

Eventually, with only a limited time left to reach Kingoonya and the train, the headlights picked out the wire gate of Eba's boundary fence. I had arrived at the "nettin'" at last. I squelched out of the jeep to open it and soon had the faithful—so far—vehicle through and the gate chained shut. Actually, it often proves fatal to stop in these circumstances instead of keeping up the momentum, and as I began to move forward again through the lake ahead, the jeep became stuck in the mud, and stopped dead. Delirious as I was, I felt that this was at least going to break the monotony, as I selected reverse gear to try to back out of it before resorting to my shovel and jack. I don't know how I would have handled them in my condition, but as if an unseen hand was being offered, the little wheels all tugging at once pulled the rest of their burden backwards and out of the bog. With no time to waste and heaving sighs of relief, I again charged it a little more quickly and this time carried on through to the higher ground on the other side.

Old established wheeltracks in the bush are always more compacted than the land alongside them even if the surrounding area is free from surface water. The mere fact that a lake can exist in the first place proves the underlying ground is solid enough to support it. On the other hand, wheeltracks slowly turn into deep ruts with a high intervening crown which can often make a vehicle "bottom".

With not much over an hour left to midnight, I tackled a long expanse of water under which the road passed, with slightly more forward surge than was needed, so that I might be carried through it without too much incident. This caused a large spray of water to flood over the bonnet, and over myself too, as being unable to operate the windscreen wiper and negotiate the mud at the same time, I had to drop the windshield. Immediately the poor little engine gave a splutter and stopped dead. This all would have been highly entertaining were it not for the throbbing lump on my face, and deadened to almost everything else, I climbed out, not worrying about getting my feet any wetter. My groans of pain were soon coming from the locality of the distributor in the engine. Protecting the operation from the rain with my dripping overcoat and thinking it might be drier in the open, I wiped the inside of the cap with my sleeve lining which wasn't quite as wet as the outside, and replaced it.

Somehow I found myself back in the driver's seat trying the switch. That invisible hand was there once more as the engine fired and after a quick look at my belt watch, I carried on as fast as I dared. If I missed the train I knew there was always that rifle alongside me which could settle anything on the spot.

By midnight the few lights in Kingoonya which were still burning came dimly into focus through the driving rain. As I crossed over the rail tracks I was conscious of the time Johnny and I had to wait for a train to pass after we'd eaten the turkey dipped in the salt water.

Switching off for the last time at the siding I slumped over the wheel to wait, hoping the train had not already passed through. It was too late to call over to the Crosbys'

Top: In 1947 Afghan George Morousen was Coober Pedy's only supplier of wood and water. He delivered to cave doorsteps. *Bottom:* For a quarter of a century, amazing Jake Santing made the 800-kilometre weekly mail run from Kingoonya to Coober Pedy. "I nursed the missus' fairy cakes on my lap all the way."

warm kitchen fire where I'm sure Doreen would have given me a mug of tea, and all I could do was just sit there rocking back and forth, hugging my jaw and concentrating on the abscess. Within half an hour, which seemed like half a week, a suggestion of a noise came to my ears from the west, and on looking along the line I detected the headlight of the steam engine dragging the transcontinental train through the pitch-black night. Fifteen minutes later it ground to a stop at the siding, and leaving my little jeep right where it was, and with no thought of a ticket or reservation of any kind, I clambered up the iron steps and collapsed on the floor inside the heavy door.

Several beautifully-dressed and perfectly dry passengers who saw me must have summoned a guard because I was soon aware of a pair of polished black shoes alongside my face. Naturally enough, I supposed when I later reconstructed all this in my mind, he enquired politely about various things which seemed to be puzzling him. Little things like where did I come from and where was my rail ticket. I managed to sit upright by leaning on the door and at the sight of my soaking form and agonised expression stemming from the pulsating mound on my jaw, he put two and two together; he had been a guard on the old "East-west" for many years and couldn't be surprised by anything that happened on this outback run.

Nothing more was mentioned about a berth and as I had a ready-made "sleeper" right where I was, I lay down again hoping we'd be at Port Augusta soon. There were only about 350 kilometres to go with no fear of bogs or stops to get through the "nettin'" and this in itself made my unorganised visit to the dentist more bearable.

At first light that morning I was aware of the train's brakes being applied amid the sounds of gushing steam and clanking, and on standing up I saw that we were at Port Augusta at last—which meant I was only a short distance from help. Lurching through the ticket collector's gateway I felt he wasn't brave enough to dare ask for a pass and I walked along the main street bent low as I held the left side of my face in a rag made wet with genuine Eba rain-

Top: The Mabel Creek cattle were hunted clear of our plane by Aboriginal guards Paddy and Billy Brown. *Bottom:* On our early survey expedition we found that Billy could also handle other airborne things in his breezy kitchen

water. It was only six o'clock with about three hours to go before anything opened in this country town, so not knowing where any dental establishment was located, I sat down on the step outside a shop to wait and suffer in what silence I could muster. An hour and a half dragged by before a serious-looking gentleman delicately stepped around me to enter his shop. This being a sort of frontier town with odd visitors from the outlying stations constantly appearing, he hardly gave me a second glance. But the sniff he gave was really unnecessary as I never touch the stuff.

On the dot of nine by my watch, I stood up and began my search by looking behind me at the door the serious gentleman had gone through one-and-a-half hours before. If I had been of a different temperament, I might have been saddened by the sign I noticed on the wall alongside the entrance. In black lettering on a huge, polished brass plate were the only words I'd been wanting to see for nearly a week: "Dental Surgeon". The serious man was in fact the dentist; if I'd known it at the time, I would have followed him in on his heels.

Three seconds was all it took me to be inside interviewing him, and he told me to sit in his waiting room until he was ready. Not wanting to emulate Banjo Paterson's "The Man from Ironbark" where the bushman wrecked the barber's shop, I sat down, groaning audibly until minutes later he softened and appeared at the door, advising me I had better come in there and then.

I sat down down in his chair, a most comfortable affair, while he proceeded to administer what I later learned to be a "mandibular block injection", even though he said it would have little effect on inflamed tissues. I was grateful I still *had* tissues, and as soon as he attacked the tooth with his lower hawksbill forceps I realised how correct was his statement about the anaesthetic having little effect. I shall never really forget the next fifteen seconds, and even now as my tongue finds the open space, I can vividly relive them one by one.

Tears were streaming down my unshaven face by the time he'd finished, and my hands were locked around his wrists. The first thing I saw when I was again able to open my eyes, was the bleary outline of my second left mandibular molar still gripped in his wonderful forceps. He was examining it under the light and pointed to the globular poison sac dangling from the end of one of the three roots. As near to total expiration as I was, the sight of it anywhere else but in my mouth gave me a feeling of elation as I released the tension which had built up over the span of the previous week. He offered me a drink of some "awkward stuff" but even then I was able to explain to him I only drank bore water. I stumbled back out into the street without worrying about his fee for I could fix all that up later. I felt free from absolute agony for the first time in many a long day.

I trudged back to the railway station to learn that the next train going west left at eight o'clock that night. To fill in the day I mooched about the waterfront where Spencer Gulf begins. Suddenly discovering it was 20 October, two days after my mother's birthday, I visited the post office to send a telegram wishing her a much happier day than I had experienced forty-eight hours before.

At eight o'clock exactly the train pulled out of Port Augusta, taking me home to Kingoonya, my jeep, and Eba. I had promised the booking clerks that after some paperwork the fare would be paid sometime later by my headquarters at Keswick. While it was still pitch black in the early hours of the next morning, the train once again came to an ear-splitting halt at Kingoonya. Climbing back down those slippery iron stairs in my hobnailed boots, I found my jeep right where I'd left it and drove it over to the Crosbys' place. At half past three in the morning everyone was understandably still asleep, but knowing where his lounge-room was even in the darkness, I crept in and lay down on his settee.

After the creaking of the floorboards under the weight of my boots had died away, I heard the ticking of the huge grandfather-clock, each tick sounding like a revolver shot in the silence. The noise was incidental compared to the inconvenience I had endured for a week so I didn't attempt to stop the persistent pendulum. Realising just how tired I was, I fell asleep in minutes. I hadn't really slept for such a long time that I was almost surprised to find how easy it was. With the coming of daybreak I crept out to my jeep and headed back to my peaceful camp at Mount Eba.

My trip back north was nothing short of beautiful, as the bright sun lit up the freshly-washed mulga trees and the clean saltbush literally sparkled in the morning air. It seemed incredible that such a transformation could occur within the space of little over a day. My overcoat thrown on the empty passenger's seat, dry bare feet on the pedals, and windscreen again upright, I felt on top of the world. The knowledge that the tooth was lying in a trash can in Port Augusta probably had something to do with the feeling of goodwill. As I passed through the receding water on the road to stop at the netting gate, I smiled when I remembered what it had been like until so very recently. Everything somehow took on a totally new aspect and in next to no time I sedately drove past the Eba homestead to my camp.

Although I couldn't tackle toast just then I felt to the full the hunger of a week as I sat down in George's kitchen to accept as much of his enticing food as I could eat. After that I was able to take out the new batch of air photos from their holders to plan the next astrofix.

Frank and I drove off a day later to locate another point on the photographs, and even though it was over 160 kilometres away to the west, we found it and were able to set up for the observations that same night. The stiff, cold wind accompanying the arrival of nightfall failed to dampen my high spirits which rubbed off on Frank, and we worked till midnight to obtain a sizeable number of star readings for an accurate position.

Admitting to rising later than usual next morning at eight o'clock, we sat around our cheerful fire while Frank was forced to listen patiently to my utterances about how it had been only two days since I'd happened to visit a faraway city.

The wind had gone by the time we left the open iron-stone flat with its one myall tree in the middle, and were bound for Eba once more. The full shadow cast by the myall when the plane had taken the photograph showed up as a black dot on the otherwise bare area, providing us with a perfect, easily-identified pinhole on the photo.

The day after we returned to camp, everyone enjoyed a Saturday excursion to Kingoonya for the annual gymkhana. "Everyone" meant just that: no station homestead for many hundreds of kilometres in any direction was inhabited at all for the weekend. Horses were driven or transported to the siding two weeks before to be stabled in the racetrack sheds, all to be fed on the same sort of grain so none would have any special advantage. Droving them for three or four hundred kilometres would be nothing out of the ordinary.

The dusty flat between Crosbys' and the railroad was strewn with the swags of bushmen who had come in, leaving the womenfolk to jostle for what little other accommodation offered. Trucks and vehicles of every description gave the appearance of a huge wrecking yard. Even a couple of Woomera trucks turned up as word of this annual event reached their ears.

All the station hands, drovers, Aborigines, managers, and children wore gaudy silk shirts of blazing reds, greens, and yellows, a commodity which Young and Gordon's store stocks up with in advance, and the day progresses amid noise and great activity as the races somehow get under way. Galloping horsemen put on exhibitions of scooping rings dangling from posts by means of a long stick held in their right hands while the controlling reins are expertly used with the left, and the one who finishes the course with the greatest number of rings threaded on his "lance" wins. Aboriginal stockmen who have a perfect seat on a saddle are often up among the winners. Silver cups, mounted riding crops, and trophies are presented, mostly donated as personal additions to the event by station owners.

We knew everyone there as we were constantly passing

151

through their stations on our work, and much good-humoured bantering was dished out to us about stargazing and claypan selection. It went on till exactly midnight. By law that was the time such things must stop and there was a man from the force present to see it was carried out, a thankless task making him the most unpopular person there; he also sorted out any fights or other disputes throughout the day.

As we drove back to Eba through the quiet blackness once more, my thoughts were still centred on how, only days before, I had left a lone jeep overnight on that same flat, while I made an out-of-the-ordinary visit to the dentist.

16

The Fix at Coober Pedy

Gladly returning to work after that most strenuous bush holiday, I next confirmed my earlier thought that there was a glaring need for an accurate astronomical latitude and longitude of the Coober Pedy opal fields, which up to now had never been fixed. Each sparse map available showed them plotted in a different place within a fifteen-kilometre radius, and as the main area appeared on the required nine air photographs and the road to Alice Springs showed up plainly, I deduced I could easily identify a point at which to carry out observations.

I first noticed the discrepancy on the different maps when I had driven 200 kilometres from Eba across gentle undulations covered with saltbush, which I had crossed so recently on our trip with the Englishmen. I used the one day between the bush race picnic and my departure from Eba in preparing another star programme, working the skins around in the tanning mixture, and packing up, the latter being something around which our lives revolved. I have often admonished myself since for ever having used a rifle on kangaroos, and now, apart from helping

Aborigines in dire need of food, I would do all I could to protect them, but in those days everything had to be put down to education.

On our way Frank and I came upon Ozzie and Harold in the middle of the rutted, corrugated highway; they had a blowout in the old three-tonner and no more spares. They had been on some photo marking-up work near Dick Rankin's Ingomar Station and after the first staked tyre they were returning to camp, but true to Ozzie's form, the truck collected another flat tyre on the way. Telling them to camp on the spot until help came, we continued on to send a message to Eba over the opal fields' Flying Doctor transceiver. Our other jeeps were scattered over the countryside where Johnny and Max were doing similar work; one of the men would drive down to collect a huge spare tyre from Woomera and take it out to the truck.

Late that afternoon we drove into Coober Pedy for my second visit. We branched off the main road on to the spur track to Young and Russell's store by the dug-out hole where they lived. Once again ominous cloud formations were rolling up from the south and by the time I would usually be setting up my theodolite, the sky was a threatening black. Thinking of what happened at the 250 Mile O.P. I went on to the tableland to pick a spot before dark.

The main road north took a right-angled turn west to Mabel Creek before resuming its direction to the Alice, and the spur track around the opal holes led off from the angle. A small thread of used wheeltracks cutting off the point showed up on the photos and joined the road twenty metres south. This point could be accurately pin-pricked so I decided to use this junction as an astronomical station. With a glance at the leaden skies, we rolled out our swags on low canvas stretchers and made a fire of saltbush roots and dry mulga sticks we'd brought on the bonnet from as far back as the Penrhyn dam, where we once slept overnight in the pouring rain. This arid country wasn't living up to its sun-baked, dusty reputation I thought, as several spots of rain began to tap on the metal bonnet of the jeep. A couple of camp-sheets covered the swags and in the space of half an hour we were huddled under them as heavy rain cascaded off the corners to form miniature lakes around the stretchers. It was good to be off the ground even if only a few centimetres, and we couldn't emerge till morning.

The bleak plains rolled out to the horizon in all directions. Although the rain had stopped the sky was as black as ever and our open jeep must have been the only object visible on that otherwise desolate, unprotected flat. Whenever I looked at such a scene, I tingled with enthusiasm at the uninhibited feeling of freedom it gave me. That morning after shaking off the canvas and briskly scanning the bare horizon, I couldn't help remarking to Frank how good it all was. I went on to say to his lashed-down camp-sheet that if my father were here he would also revel in it and burst out with his favourite saying "My word! What a country!" Frank peeled back a corner of his canvas shelter and dragged his gaze around the same dreary, sodden spectacle, replying gloomily that if his mother were here she would shut out the landscape with her hand over her eyes and groan "My word, what a country!"

A fire was almost impossible to start and even then we had nothing much to cook. So leaving the beds standing starkly alone on the desert, we sloshed the jeep in four-wheel drive through the mud down to Jack Young and Harry Russell's comparatively luxurious establishment 200 metres away in the hollow. With them in the snug little dirt cave were the owners of a foreign vehicle we had seen the previous evening. Everyone knew every motor car in the country and a strange one caused much comment and speculation; in this case there was plenty of cause for it all.

Sitting at the wooden table, each with his mug of tea, were three men whom we'd never seen before and who were relatively well dressed for this area. A tiger shooter's pith helmet lay upside down on a tea-chest by the table. We were soon introduced to the director and producer of a documentary film currently being shot in the outback and with them was a travelling minister whose parish extended from Port Augusta to Alice Springs. As we wolfed down the proffered mugs of tea, we gathered that the film was to deal with the lifesaving Flying Doctor network over the back country, and would be released under the title of *Mantle of Safety*. I happened to glance into the pith helmet and was amazed to notice the name "Kingsford Smith" printed in ink on the inside of the crown, so I asked about it. The man who had formed the Kingcroft film company in Sydney claimed ownership, revealing that he was in fact a nephew of the famous Sir Charles. You certainly don't meet many people in the bush, but when you do they very often turn out to be quite exciting. So here we all were sheltering from the elements like cavemen in one of the most barren sections of countryside you can find on the road to the Alice.

Their filming had been delayed by the weather at Coober Pedy where they had secured a sequence of Mrs Russell using her transceiver, which she did daily from a special radio hole in the ground. The aerial stood above ground with the leads trailing into the ventilation hole through the roof, and the square of calico pinned to the dirt above the set stopped loose particles from raining down on to the array of knobs. I later visited the studios in Sydney where the film was being edited and was shown footage relating to our unusual meeting on the opal fields.

The whole day was occupied mainly by sheltering from the wind which had sprung up during the morning, and came whistling unobstructed across the plains. This gave us a chance to struggle from dugout to dugout to meet the rest of the inhabitants. The cave alongside Young and Russell's was currently being used by Mr Kingsford Smith and party, so we gave up the idea of temporarily shifting camp from our present site, swept by wind and rain. This cave was owned by old Jake Santing, the Dutch mail-driver whose run extended from Kingoonya through all the stations to Coober Pedy. He stayed in his opal field "residence" when he arrived on his weekly visits. Every time it rained anywhere in this country, the resulting discussions invariably ended up with " . . . and old Jake got bogged", a foregone conclusion even if the news hadn't actually circulated on the radio waves.

Jake, a hunchback, was nearly seventy when I knew him, bent over double, weather-beaten and as brown as a berry, with a string of tales and legends surrounding him that no other bushman since Ned Kelly had collected. His old truck was a tangled mass of fencing wire holding on such incidental parts as mudguards and bonnet and I'm sure the top speed was not much more than twenty-five kilometres an hour. One woman at the opal fields had ordered a box of fairy cakes for a special occasion to be brought up the 300 kilometres by Jake, so he duly collected them from the "Tea and Sugar" train at Kingoonya. The truck was loaded to its limits with diesel fuel, drums of petrol and sheep dip, parts for windmills, and every conceivable item of merchandise for the stations, so Jake placed the iced cakes on the seat alongside him. The rough parts of the road kept making the box fall on to the floor among the old dingo scalps and jars of strychnine used for laying baits on the way, so he tossed it back on to a drum of dieseline. The drum it landed on unfortunately had a leaky bung which Jake discovered when unloading some goods at a homestead. The box was swimming in a pool of fuel so he thoughtfully transferred it on to a four-gallon tin of sheep dip. There it bounced about in the blazing sun for three days until he approached his destination. Four hundred metres out of Coober Pedy he pulled up, climbed laboriously to the top of his load, threw the unfortunate box of dainty goodies to the ground, and travelled the remaining stone's throw with it sedately balanced on his knees.

As soon as the lumbering old truck rattled to a stop in a voluminous cloud of red bulldust outside the store, the naïve woman was there at his door to collect her parcel. Jake handed it over and, with a bland expression on his weather-beaten face, assured her that he had "nursed it on his lap all the way". The sun-baked, rock-hard fairy cakes, still supporting most of their pink icing, were at least softened in the lower half by the diesel fuel, but the overall smell of sheep dip was enough to make anyone knock them back.

Cheques for very large sums could be found stuffed down under the old seat in the cabin, worn thin and sometimes held together with hardened lumps of dust-impregnated grease, but Jake would only mumble that he'd clear them out sometime. One day as he trundled on to Eba airstrip to collect some goods from the plane, he struggled out of the cabin and, placing one hand on the wire holding the mudguards together, swivelled his head from his hunched-over stance to look at me. I had met him and was staring at the heap of scrap he called a truck, its engine open to view complete with jam tins over open oil vents. As I contemplated the travelling wreck he pointed out in a resigned voice, "It is falling to pieces on me". I couldn't help but politely agree, adding quickly that it was still a goer, before he shuffled, head down, towards the plane. Just as I looked up he was going straight for the razor-sharp leading edge of one of the stationary propellers, but I was too late to shout a warning. With all the momentum of his strongly-built body behind it, the shiny, bald crown of his head smashed against the blade, splitting his skin open for at least seven centimetres. Blood, thinned by the blazing heat of the sun, cascaded out to soak the red dust below.

Almost as though nothing had happened, he continued on to the open door of the plane and shouldered a large box over to his vehicle. Only after it had been dumped on his truck did he wipe off the surplus blood with his dirty sleeve and hold a piece of rag over it so it wouldn't trickle into his eyes as he climbed behind the wheel. Shaped as he was, he drove with the upper part of his back halfway down the seat in order to allow his face to be directed towards the windscreen.

He had been pushing a wreck of a mail truck, after his previous camel-wagon days, over the same route for nearly a quarter of a century. This truck was finally replaced with an old army "blitz buggy". While I was there he finally gave up and sold out to Tom Young, Jack's brother. I met him by accident on a street in Adelaide years later and had a long yarn with him, which proved to be the last time I ever saw him. Reports filtered quickly around the outback that old Jake, one of the last really genuine bush mail-drivers, had finally died, and with him went the thousands of stories which had taken him a long hard lifetime to accumulate.

We'd already sent the radio message for the tyre needed by Ozzie and late afternoon was approaching, so we ploughed our way back to our airy bedroom to be on hand in case the stars decided to appear. But there was no hope of observing throughout the wild night of howling wind and intermittent rain, and back we went to the dugout in the morning. Some of that day was spent lying at the bottom of a twelve-metre opal shaft and digging into the walls with a geological hammer, with no results as usual. Kingsford Smith and his party remained crouched out of the weather. As our hurricane oil lamp burnt out of fuel, we edged our way back to the surface by the footholds gouged into the sides of the hole.

As night fell we didn't even bother to report to our lone beds as the wind and rain had not let up all day. Instead we sat yarning in Harry Russell's cave, and at midnight we still had no inclination to rush back to our wind-battered sleeping area. Then Jack Young, who was born into a store-keeping family, suddenly commented on the fact that there was no signboard on their store. I replied that as I had a signwriter's brush and white paint I would make them one, but the problem was where to find a board on which to do the lettering. Harry solved that immediately when he said there was a loose tail-board on Bert Wilson's truck at The Eight Mile, so there and then we jumped in the jeep and went off through the storm on our mission. As the rain and wind lashed down on us we disconnected the part in question from Bert's truck and by three o'clock in the morning we were sitting around it back in the dugout.

Still not anxious to repair to our bedroom, I took out the paint and brush. By the first indication of dawn, as gloomy as it still was, the finished sign was ready to nail up outside the tin store, reading "Young and Russell—Store" in large capital letters. During the day Bert chugged into the main fields and the first comment he made on entering the store was directed at the new sign. All efforts to distract him failed to prevent him wondering where his tail-board had dropped off.

The weather was foul and looked as if it had set in forever, but that night we crawled into our moistened bed rolls. We hadn't seen them for two days and the wind had driven the rain underneath the canvas.

The sound of a motor woke us in the early morning and we peeped out to see the Kingsford Smith film van driving off westward on the Mabel Creek road; it had stopped raining and the wind had abated overnight. Black clouds still crowded the sky as we saw the truck dwindle in size, but as we watched, some drops of rain hit our faces followed by more, and soon the downpour was on again. We both thought of it together: Jake's dugout! We began tossing our swags on to the jeep, bent on at last being able to sleep out of the incessant bad weather, but when we cast a glance towards the truck, to our horror we saw it was in the act of turning around. We could have easily beaten them to it but just didn't have the heart. Their van grew bigger and bypassed us on its way back to their dugout shelter. We later learned that they had decided to make the break but when the rain started they quickly scurried back to the one known shelter in hundreds of thousands of square kilometres.

Another day of waiting passed and amazingly after dark that night the wind dropped, the sky cleared, and a hemisphere of brilliant stars was revealed at long last. Using it to the full, I stood at the theodolite observing until well past midnight.

At first light we were up and had the evening's star readings calculated by early afternoon, giving us the first accurate geographical position of the Coober Pedy opal fields. Now when I occasionally pass through the fields, the memory of that astrofix recurs crystal clear in my mind's eye. On the very spot where we camped in the open during that wild week in 1947, a two-storeyed hotel has been

160

built to house tourists who would otherwise have to sleep unprotected from the elements—or in Jake's dugout, providing it was vacant.

Heading off towards Mabel Creek as soon as we'd packed up, we located another photo point where a waterway crossed the road. Usually dry, at present it was a banker with water stained with yellow mud. Another full astronomical night followed, and as we were only twenty-seven kilometres away, we went back to the dugout to do the calculations. Finishing up with another latitude and longitude printed on the back of the air photos alongside a circle drawn around the pin-prick, we began to feel the need of a night's sleep for a change. We rolled out our swags, without a conscience this time, on the floor of Jake's dugout; he was still bogged after the rains near the Penrhyn according to the radio. On the way back to the fields we stopped to wash our grimy shirts and shorts in a rainwater puddle just off the muddy road, and had a bath by the simple means of just lying down in it. At the Eight Mile we had a mug of tea on Bert's claim, carefully steering the conversation away from his missing tail-board.

While we were sitting there, a full-blood Aboriginal opal gouger (strictly not digger) ambled in from his simmering old buckboard with a cloth bag held up in either hand. The bottom half of the legs of his old riding trousers had been hacked off, indicating where he had obtained the bags, the ends of which were tied in a knot. Bert had a tattered card-table unfolded near by and the Aboriginal, without a word of explanation, walked over and dumped the bags on the dusty green top. Taking up one by the knot he emptied out the entire contents and tossed the bag on to the dirt, repeating the operation with the other. There, to our utter astonishment, lay a cone-shaped pile of pure opal, gleaming in the light of the candles. We stared at it speechlessly, but Bert merely grunted and mooched over to study the treasure.

Scarcely able to breathe, we approached the bonanza and gingerly held up a hunk the size of a table-tennis ball to gaze in awe at the fire it was emitting. In the glimmer of

161

the candle, rays of red, green, and yellow burst out into the darkness. Becoming braver, we took up piece after piece from the most beautiful mound of stones we had ever seen in our lives, to hold each in wonder close to the flickering light. It turned out that the Aboriginal had climbed down a hole sunk years before, lit a kerosene lamp, and started gouging. Just beyond where the last prospector had stopped he struck this pocket of pure opal, over three centimetres thick and at least forty-five centimetres across, which literally tumbled out with every blow of his pick on the underlying chocolate opal dirt. Whipping out his knife he sawed off the legs of his trousers which he knotted, then proceeded to fill by shovelling in the fabulous gemstones with his hand. Penniless, he had climbed down the hole at two o'clock that afternoon when we'd been washing our shirts in the desert, and he had emerged at four, thousands of pounds richer.

Out came a rusty pair of kitchen scales and after some calculations, Bert offered him £2,000 for the "parcel" on the spot. In the days before the opal explosion when prices skyrocketed, that offer sounded to our untrained ears a gigantic figure and very fair indeed, as it did to the grinning Aboriginal who accepted it. But where, we wondered, was that sort of money to be obtained on these treeless, prehistoric gibber plains. As if he read our thoughts, Bert answered that in the following minute by kneeling down beside his hessian-topped bed made of bush sticks threaded through woolpacks, and groped blindly underneath. A scraping sound followed as a rusty kerosene tin was dragged out, bulldozing a miniature mound of dirt along with it, and his free hand dipped into the ragged top which had been removed with a tin opener. Our eyes opened even wider as handfuls of £10 notes were extracted and dropped alongside in the dust.

Counting was the next operation, and afterwards the gouger, sporting a wide, toothless grin, walked back into the sunlight, with his tattered pockets bulging as well as his two fists. One huge bundle of notes tied with string fell out of his shirt pocket on to the ground in front of him,

162

and he kicked it across the stones to his buckboard with his toe.

Back in the gloom Bert began searching for his bent old pair of glasses as we rummaged through the mountain on the table. He called over his shoulder for each of us to select a lump as a present, and added as an afterthought two minutes later from a darkened corner where he was feeling in vain for his glasses, "Not too big though." There's absolutely nothing on earth like Australian bush people.

The next time I saw the lucky Aboriginal he was wearing a full set of new teeth from the store, a brightly-coloured sports coat, and light grey slacks under which his bare feet protruded. He didn't want to go completely mad on his spending spree in Port Augusta, but a sparkling new travelling suitcase held a large assortment of gay silk shirts for his tribe. We drove off a little later with our precious pair of gemstones wrapped in our best piece of rag, nestling in a corner of the theodolite box, the safest spot on the whole jeep.

Jake's dugout proved to be a most sheltered and snug bedroom. We converted it into a computing office the next morning and didn't emerge until the last sum had been finished.

Before going to another observation point on our way back to Eba, we couldn't resist the temptation to implore Harry Russell to let us drive his ancient Model T Ford. The wonderful old vintage creation standing outside the store was still in working condition. After the spluttering engine was started, I soon wedged myself behind the huge wooden steering wheel and worked the hand throttle levers, slowly depressing the band clutch pedal. I'm sure I'll never drive anything as exhilarating as that car. Returning it to the store to the cheers of the gathering I remembered having found a number plate on the road on the way up. I asked Harry if it perhaps belonged to this unregistered, numberless Ford, but he denied ownership immediately, stating that it was far too much extra weight for the old girl to carry.

As we left this amazing settlement behind, obscured by the dust which had quickly replaced the mud, we felt really honoured and fortunate that our work had brought us to such an incredible place.

17

The End of
the Beginning

As if to make quite sure we weren't too long without
entertainment, we were involved in another exciting drama
just one day after returning to Eba, while we were still
working out the results of the star observations we'd
taken.

I was sitting at George's kitchen table poring over open
nautical almanacs and books of mathematical tables,
deeply engrossed in the sums. Suddenly Bob Crombie's
eight-year-old son, Barry, burst in to break the news
coming over their Flying Doctor transceiver. A civilian
Dakota aircraft, full of passengers from Alice Springs
bound for Adelaide, was in trouble. One engine, although
not actually on fire, had registered alarm readings on the
instrument panel before coughing to a grinding halt. Right
now the engine was smoking hot, and with its propellers
feathered the stricken aeroplane was limping over the
saltbush plains east of Coober Pedy about 150 kilometres
north of Eba, on its one remaining engine. All twin-
engined aircraft are built to be able to fly on only one
motor, but with the intense heat of the mid-November

desert causing considerable turbulence, it would be much safer to have both working at once.

As we rushed up to the homestead, the radioed messages indicated that the plane was gradually losing height and we knew it would soon be over a belt of heavy mulga scrub which would make any sort of forced landing impossible. Of course they were desperately trying to make the distance to the airstrip at Eba which was normally a routine stop; it was a calculated risk to attempt the mulga belt leaving behind the last hope of landing on an open gibber plain. At that minute the pilots had decided to make the try.

We assured them over the transceiver that we were standing by with our jeeps in the event of any last-minute ditching operation, and requested constant information as to their location. Their radio operator was well aware that if they reached our strip we would be on hand at the landing. The minutes dragged by and reports of the scenery below the plane were enough for us to know almost exactly where they were all the time, as we had covered every centimetre of that country in the course of our survey work. A mention of a sheoak patch or an angle in a fence line were enough to allow us to plot their positions. If any failure in their radio occurred or if they made a sudden announcement that they were coming down, we could head off accurately across country to where we last heard from them.

The burning heat of the country at that time of year made any sort of travelling an ordeal at best, and it must have been an explosive atmosphere on board because we were tensed-up just listening to their reports, but the longer they kept coming, the closer they would be to us, and eventually it seemed as if they would actually reach the strip. As we listened, their navigator broke in with the news to the radio operator that Mount Eba homestead was then actually in sight. Leaving someone at the transceiver, we burst outside and in a matter of a minute, the drone of an aeroplane engine wafted over the quiet mulga trees to us. Tumbling into our jeeps we streaked over to the airfield

166

as the Dakota came into sight. With its undercarriage already down it made a direct approach, disregarding the usual circling inspection of the wind-sock and a glance over the dirt runway for stray horses or sheep. They had obviously had enough excitement and were eager to bring the adventure to a close as quickly as possible.

The wing tips exaggerated the effect of the hot ground thermals as the plane was lifted and dropped by them, and appeared anything but level or steady, but at least it was coming down here and not over a sea of hard mulga trees. One set of propellers was labouring gallantly while the port set was quite stationary. Within the next minute the lucky aeroplane was settled on the wonderful, solid ground, shimmering like a huge silver jelly in the mirage.

We were right there by the door as it opened and the sweating passengers spilled out with various expressions of relief. One young man, more light-hearted and obviously the comedian of the group, knelt down on his hands and knees in full view of everyone and kissed the hot dirt with a flourish as though he were facing Mecca.

Much exuberant bantering followed in the wake of the subsiding tension, as the passengers gradually lost their former petrified appearance. Someone even remarked brightly that we now had enough people for a cricket match. We ferried them all over to the homestead with their belongings, as they were certainly not going to re-enter that particular machine, and Flo prepared the usual scones and gallons of tea to cope with them all. In their city clothing they looked quite out of place in these parts, but at least they were all alive.

Radio messages were already being sent to the airline concerned in Adelaide and another plane was being pre-pared to leave on the following morning, bound for Eba. The overnight delay was due to the time taken in arranging for a replacement engine and aircraft fitters to be on board, and the same plane would of course take on all the passengers to resume their journey.

Mount Eba somehow looked different for the rest of the day as clean-looking people in polished shoes and lipstick wandered about, looking over an outback sheep station probably for the first and last time in their lives. One man, obviously a botanist, spent his time collecting specimens of saltbush and a large variety of herbage that we didn't even know existed. Their evening meal was already being prepared by George, and whatever it was, I knew they were in for a treat.

Shearers' quarters, homestead verandahs, and woolshed were to be their bedrooms with priority given to women-folk, who would sleep at the house. After tea in the cool of the long twilight the idea of the cricket match was put into effect. Barry and Robert's bats were brought out and the men challenged our survey camp to play. Nobody won, as the botanist was more intent on examining specimens while fielding than chasing the ball, but once, as he was looking hard at a small leaf structure, a haymaker swipe at the ball by Ozzie connected, sending it streaking towards his face. Just in time he saw it and, dropping the leaf, raised his hands to protect himself; the hurtling missile landed in his open palms two centimetres from his nose and Ozzie was out for a duck. Afterwards at tea we remarked on what a spectacular catch it was, only to receive his nonchalant reply: "After all that's what I was there for."

At dawn the second plane appeared and a tubular scaffold brought for the purpose was assembled, soon to have the replacement engine dangling from its strong, endless chain hoist. The small wheels at the feet of the framework, which were designed for sealed hardstandings at city airports, just sank into the red dust and refused to roll the heavy load out of the doorway. Anticipating this, I already had my jeep and tow rope waiting and we towed it clear of the plane, while the spare seats on board were anchored to their usual mounts. The passengers had all been ferried over with their belongings and were bunched around watching the proceedings. In a matter of minutes they were installed with seat belts firmly adjusted as the pilots were driven back to their aircraft from Flo Crombie's traymobile of scones and tea at the house. With engines roaring, the plane, which although small by normal airline standards still looked huge to us out here in the bush, slewed around, pelting us with dust and ironstone gravel, to face the open flat.

They buzzed us after take-off, level with the tops of the mulgas, and straightened out in the direction of Adelaide, leaving the original pilots and fitters to restore the crippled craft. Apparently for psychological reasons, pilots aren't supposed to see what goes on in the mechanical operation of repairing or replacing parts, so we willingly volunteered our help to the fitters. With the engine swinging below, I towed the makeshift structure across the saltbush, gouging deep ruts in the dirt, and finally deposited the new machine on the ground under the wing, leaving the crane free to take on the useless motor when it was detached. The weight was taken and the maze of wires and tubes was unscrewed, finishing up with the removal of the main holding bolts which allowed the heavy machine to swing freely. We towed the whole apparatus around to the door in the fuselage and manoeuvred it inside, working the chains to place the engine where it would be firmly strapped to the floor for its return down south.

The laborious operation continued by attaching the new one to the crane, and dragging it into place alongside the gaping hole in the wing left by the other engine. Bolts were replaced after much microscopic adjustment of the hoist, and the task of joining up the multitude of loose ends began.

By early afternoon the whole concern once more resembled an aeroplane and the pilots were collected to take it for a test flight in which we were invited to participate. As we screamed along the strip to the critical moment of take-off, I kept thinking of those few flimsy bolts holding that huge, thundering motor in place, and realised why the pilots themselves don't usually have anything to do with the mechanical side of flying. After crawling over the outback like snails in our comparatively slow jeeps, the speed of take-off seemed supersonic to us and soon we were circling over the homestead and woolshed as the pilots lined up for a landing, satisfied that it all worked once more.

They stayed long enough for the mobile scaffolding to be taken apart and loaded, after which, by now our firm friends, they lit out for Adelaide as if nothing had happened. Apart from joining up a thousand wires and tubes in the right places, there was really nothing to putting a new engine in an aeroplane and we felt we were learning something every day. After all, you never know when you'll be called upon to put an engine in an aeroplane.

Soon after this slight interruption the astronomical calculations were finished, and I was free to head off the following day for another star fix 160 kilometres away in the sandhills west of Dick Rankin's Ingomar homestead. It was a perfect night for the observations, which kept me going into the early hours of the morning, leaving a few hours to sleep in my swag before driving back. This was the last necessary position for our map and had to be done before we could all leave Eba and return to the Purple Downs woolshed area. Word had come to us that some special series of large-scale maps were needed around the Woomera locality as work progressed, to enable detailed planning of the various future bombing and short missile ranges which were now coming into the picture.

This meant that we would shift camp to be more central to our new scene of operations, while we extended our original trig survey to cover the enlarged area with a network of accurate points from which we could produce the new maps. "Yandandaree Special" and "Pimba Special" were the first two required, and the "Purple woolshed" was willingly made available by Norman Greenfield as it was unoccupied between the annual shearing seasons.

Before pulling out from Eba I had to mend the tyre of my jeep which had deflated in one second as I neared the camp on the main road after the last star observation. It had taken a little time to stop from a speed of eighty kilometres an hour, and the flat tyre made the slowing-down process quite exciting as it slewed the jeep back and forth across the road over the loose dust and gravel. My inspection revealed an exact disc cut out of the tube, .303 inches in diameter, and the brass case of the heavy rifle cartridge was still embedded halfway through the canvas and rubber tread. How these things penetrate the thick tyre cover has always been a mystery, as it would be quite impossible to hammer the thin brass shell through, even if we tried all day.

Knowing we'd all be back eventually, we slowly drove out of Mount Eba Station. I was sure the one who would be missed most would be George, by now the established station cook. At Kingoonya there was a hitch in the journey while Harold brought Doreen up to date with all the latest news, and the people in the siding wanted us to play cricket. They had heard of the plane passengers' match of course, and it had given them something to plan for ever since. I struggled on slowly to East Well with the old three-ton blitz truck and spent the night with Joe and his family, cutting their hair and rehearsing our progress with the stockwhip.

The others caught up next morning and we all drove sadly through Woomera which by now had mushroomed with shacks and tents; the atmosphere of the area as we had known it earlier in the year had gone forever. Everyone there had heard of us "hillbillies from the sticks", and already we seemed to have become a legend as curious newcomers gathered around our tired old vehicles from the bush.

We carried on past the Ponds for we preferred to camp at our old bog hole at Paradise Well rather than in the metropolis, leaving only forty-two kilometres to go to reach the Purple woolshed. By the following midday we were installed there with several tents erected outside because the shearers' quarters made us feel too cooped up, and George had a fire going in the bread-baking oven built into the rockwork in the kitchen shed.

It was only then that we discovered the disappearance of a .22 rifle from Mick's jeep and a thorough search for it

171

proved fruitless. This was a very serious matter for it belonged to the army, and Wally had to cover himself by submitting a report written by Mick to Keswick which might even save him a court-martial. The rifle had definitely been in his jeep as far as Kingoonya and that was the last anyone had seen of it. During the cricket match someone must have decided it was too attractive to leave lying about, and we agreed they wouldn't have taken it if they hadn't wanted it for some good reason. Wally asked Mick to give his written statement a title, and in due course it was delivered to the military police at headquarters. They read it out just as Mick had written it: "About the rifle that was supposed to be in the truck . . . "

The first task was to establish a new network of trig stations which could be connected to our main chain covering Woomera, and this work began immediately. New points were located and more of Brooks' old stations were discovered, and eventually the actual theodolite work could start with the observations of hundreds of angles between the beacons.

The Purple Downs children weren't idle for any weekend afterwards for many months to come as I collected them to help in finding the original old sites, saving the more interesting and mysterious ones for Saturdays and Sundays when they were free from correspondence school work.

Weeks of concentrated work followed, preparing and sighting trig beacons, observing angles at first light in the mornings and just before dusk. This avoided the incessant mirage and heat shimmer which made it absolutely impossible to work with a theodolite at other times. Metal vanes, sixty centimetres in diameter, which would normally be seen through the telescope as a steady pinhead-sized black dot on the highest part of an undulation on the skyline, would during the day appear to melt into the boiling, liquid haze on the horizon which obliterated the whole undulation itself.

This more often than not meant sleeping on the spot, alongside a tripod erected in readiness for the attachment of the instrument as soon as the eastern sky showed signs of the approaching new day. A relatively short period of time was available before the sun again transformed the country into a swimming liquid. Battery-operated lights with precisely-shaped reflectors were the ideal answer for the reading of all these angles after dark, but this involved a second party on a distant trig station to man them, a thing which we didn't always have.

Woomera now had the privilege of the company of a small band of those wonderful men from the Salvation Army who are always present at such places, and one day we received word that they even had a film showing scheduled. A large, white canvas tent fly was erected by a willing group of workers on a slope near our old escarpment and a projector was set up on a camp table, operated by a diesel generator placed far enough away so that it wouldn't blot out the sound effects with its noise.

We drove to the escarpment as we planned to be reading some angles at Pearson's Hill on the morning after the big night at the "theatre". By the time we got there it was already dark. Allowing the jeep to gradually roll down behind the assembled group, consisting of the entire population of Woomera at the time, we were the only ones sitting down on seats with back rests as we didn't even have to get out of our vehicle. Johnny and I couldn't believe that we were really at a drive-in cinema on this tableland. Throughout the film I could merely glance up and over the screen to watch the passage of the stars, for once not having to use them for an astrofix.

At the close of this historic evening we hurriedly backed the jeep away from the patrons and lit out across the open plains to camp at Pearson's Hill.

The pace of this work kept up at full speed despite the intense heat of the approaching summer months (it was now December), and constant high winds and dust storms battered our little camp by the woolshed. We rarely slept at the same spot two nights running but lay down wherever we happened to be at nightfall, on sandhills, gibber plains, and in occasional patches of mulga scrub. At last I could sleep throughout the desert nights without the never-ending need for star observations which had made me a slave to the heavens for so long. Those requirements would surely return and I would tackle them without reluctance, but at the same time the novelty of a full night's rest was as good as a holiday.

Christmas was approaching and a few weeks' cessation of work was imminent, so I planned to bring the surveys up to a point from which I could continue in the new year, and with this goal in mind I felt I must not waste a single minute. A fortnight short of Christmas Day we all packed up our few meagre belongings, the instruments, and the field books which in themselves were more valuable than everything else put together, and leaving the tents where they were in readiness for our return, we farewelled our Purple Downs friends and slowly moved off towards Woomera.

We straggled into Port Augusta that night and at the expense of Wally Relf, slept for almost the first time that year under a roof and in a regular bed, without the need for a canvas-covered swag roll.

Such a year couldn't have so easy a conclusion, I thought, as I drove the old three-tonner out of the Port next morning. My theory proved correct as I started the drive over Horrock's Pass in the southern Flinders Ranges on our way back to Keswick. Halfway up the long, steep incline my engine literally exploded as the pulley wheel with its snapped stub of shaft flew off from the generator, to be pulled in by the fan belt and smashed through the radiator core. It was the last straw for our faithful old truck and I was able to allow it to roll back by gravity to a spot where I could turn it around, pointing once more back to Port Augusta twenty-five kilometres away. This was more like it, trouble to the end. I was almost relieved as I let the big vehicle roll down to the bottom of the pass where one of our jeeps could tow it back for help. The same trouble happening a week before would have meant coping with it ourselves, where the only help available was to be found at the end of our own arms.

This, then, brought to a close the first year in the development of what has often been referred to as the best testing range in the world, and the start of a project of such importance and magnitude that it is still flourishing now, well over a quarter of a century later. It has been the life employment of many thousands of people and their families, and the scene of the joy and tragedies which accompany any community. Woomera is the birthplace of hundreds of Australians, and the final resting place of the many whose lives have come to their conclusion out there on the gibber and saltbush plains that we first knew merely as "the Ponds". People have begun lifelong partnerships, marrying in the churches, and "Woomeraites" have become friends of the strongest kind, living as they did and still do in their unique town, safely clear of the approach funnel to the aerodrome which helped to govern the very location in the first place, so long before.

It has led directly to the opening up, for the first time, of the remaining 2.6 million square kilometres of virtually unexplored and unknown country in Central and Western Australia, and countless thousands of people have already benefited in various ways by the use of our 6500-kilometre network of roads covering it. My discovery of Hairy Lolly's remote tribe west of the Gibson Desert was but one of the multitude of highlights which have crowded my own life's work since being given the privilege of starting off in the field a project of such gigantic proportions.

I have been constantly grateful for the incredible good fortune which ultimately steered me to that mantelpiece in Melbourne where I was asked to go over and start "some sort of a rocket range—or something".